Gullah/Geechee:

Africa's Seeds in...

By Queen Quet Marquetta L. Goodwine

Kinship Publications

For years I walked these streets and each and every time, my feet burned. I got boils on the bottoms as the stones and concrete would heat up. I saw my ancestors.

I did not want to go back into the center of this place that was so heavily weighted with the pain, suffering, and exploitation that it was built on and that now creeps out from all the facades that have been placed on top of it to make it pretty to tourists. I heard my ancestors.

I heard my ancestors speak to me one day as I walked from the port where they had been brought from Sullivan's Island to be sold here in the midst of the streets. Some of them were bare to the world. All that they owned now showed to those who would bid on the black cargo that would create for them gold.

I found myself now turning a corner that I normally did not go down. I looked on the sign and saw that I was on Queen Street. I smiled.

The pain slowly crept in and crept up as I walked on. I had learned to change shoes in order to ease the occurrence, but this had not changed the fact that my feet burned.

This day as the pain crept in I then found myself on cobble- stone. As I touched it, I could feel the boils beginning to form. I could feel the discomfort and I thought of how this was coming through the soles of my shoes, but what was coming through the souls of my people was more painful. They had walked with nothing on their feet. They had walked at a hotter time of year. They had walked this same route.

I got back to my room and I heard my ancestors.

I heard every word that they had been speaking to me as I walked and my feet burned and I walked. I sat in the water and tried to sooth the pain and it seemed to intensify until I started to write of their torture and how they were stripped of their dignity in order to make them the right kind of "item" for sale to another.

They pointed out to me how Chalmers Street was not the place where they were stood. They were stood right here in the open in the midst of these streets. This was considered town business. They were the items of exchange.

I heard them scream! I heard the children cry! I heard the many tongues all speaking at once and wanting simply to break the chains and pull their brothers and sisters back from amongst these sick ones that would dare to gather and watch.

I saw their eyes as they pierced my soul and forever branded it as they had been branded right after the "slave coins" had been exchanged. They were dragged away.

They told me-TELL THEM!!! TELL THEM!!! OUR CHILDREN-TELL THEM!!!!

They told me in many tongues and as on the Day of Pentecost, I under and overstood them all. None were uncommon to me and none were unknown.

As the ocean's waves seemed to come up to cover and erase this scene. I gave my word that I would. Herein begins the homage to these ancestral souls that became the mortar of the city of Charles Town as their blood, sweat, and tears went into the cobblestones that they carried from the ships that brought them in and these became the pavement on which their feet heated up and bled. This is where their blood spilled when they looked someone in the eye and was beaten, when they fought back and were hung, when they cut themselves as they swung blades to fight back for their own right to the tree of life.

As I walked each pulsation of that blood connected with me and embedded new life as if my genes had been spliced. Their blood, my blood, our blood speaks and still holds together, Cha'stun.

Gullah/Geechee:
Africa in the Winds of the Diaspora
Volume IV:
Cha'stun an E Islandts

By Queen Quet Marquetta L. Goodwine
©2006 Queen Quet Marquetta L. Goodwine

Kinship Publications

Contact the

Gullah/Geechee Sea Island Coalition

Post Office Box 1207

St. Helena Island SC 29920

843-838-1171 • GullGeeCo@aol.com

www.gullahgeechee.net

For additional copies of this book or to purchase any of the following books, CDs, or DVDs by the author go to **www.gullahgeechee.biz**.

- *Gullah/Geechee: Africa's Seeds in the Winds of the Diaspora*

    Volume I: St. Helena's Serenity

    Volume II: Gawd Dun Smile Pun Wi:

Beaufort Isles

Volume III: *Frum Wi Soul Tuh de Soil: The Sea Island Cash Crops-Cotton, Rice, and Indigo*

Volume IV: 365-366

- *The Legacy of Ibo Landing: Gullah Roots of African American Culture*

- *Tinkin' 'Bout Famlee: A Geechee Down Novella* by Ronald and Marquetta L. Goodwine

- *Brother and Sister...Heart to Heart* by Ronald and Marquetta L. Goodwine

- *WEBE Gullah/Geechee: Cultural Capital & Collaboration Anthology*

- CD: *"Hunnuh Hafa Shout Sumtime!!!"*

- CD: *"Hunnuh Chillun"*

- CD: *"Cum Een"*

- CD: *"Sea Island Soul"*

- DVD: *The Gullah*

Gullah/Geechee:
Africa in the Winds of the Diaspora
Volume IV:
Cha'stun an E Islandts

Dedication

"We cannot lift ourselves up by mere complaint, adverse criticism and condemnation. We must exhibit to the world more and more each day tangible, visible, indisputable evidences of our progress and work to the country."

• Booker T. Washington September 12, 1901 at Thompson Auditorium on Rutledge Avenue in Charleston in an address to over 3000 blacks.

As has been the tradition of my people, I was sent to school to learn the way that westerners thought and their ways in the world. When I went to school or anywhere in public, I took my entire community with me. Thus, I was not to disrespect them or act as if I had "no home training."

The home training is what brought me full circle to realizing that they never sent us to school in order to be changed into others, but to be better at being who God created us to be. We were to then in turn give more to the community and to the family that nurtured us. This would no doubt make the community better than it had been. So, if one of us got better, we all got better. Just as when one mourned, we all mourned.

I do not mourn my ancestors because I know that their spirits are still with me. I mourn the coming of children who have people as their caretakers that do not want to look at from whence they came and do not want to admit who they are and from whence the roots of their families stem.

I do not mourn my ancestors. I celebrate them and my elders. I honor them. Thus, this book is dedicated to all of them and to the Gullah/ Geechee Nation where the Gullah/Geechee Nation stood together to tell the world "WE ARE A NATION! WI SPEAK FA WI!"

I dedicate this work to my mother that insured that we went to school just as her mother wanted her and her siblings to do. She did not realize just how much more we learned at home.

I dedicate this to Kumar who shows each day how much he is learning at home and how his "mother wit" comes forth even in a basic conversation about choices that people are making that they should not make.

I dedicate this to Elder Carlie Towne, Elder Lesa Wineglass-Smalls, Elder Ernestine Tobias Felder, and all those that stand by me and with me as we continue to work to complete the process of reconstruction that was begun by my ancestors here in the Gullah/Geechee Nation. Disya fa hunnuh chillun!

"The institution of slavery in all of its varied forms is one of the most idiosyncratic practices found in all of human history. Throughout time, practically all of the world's civilizations and cultures have experienced some type of slavery, and peoples both ancient and modern in societies ranging from the simplest to the most complex have coped with the practice and with the many manifestations of its legacy. In a seemingly dichotomous world, the presence of slavery has occasionally served to fashion a meaning for freedom by defining such an attribute through its negation. So it is difficult to try to understand the modern world without considering one of the most perplexing elements of the human condition. Making sense of slavery, and all of its associated elements and consequences, encompasses much of human history."
(Encyclopedia of World Slavery, Rodriguez, xiii)

Introduction

The Gullah/Geechee exist from Jacksonville, North Carolina to Jacksonville, Florida in the Sea Islands and Lowcountry of the United States of America. The area that gave life to this culture is now the "Gullah/Geechee Nation." This nation's founding cornerstone is stained with the blood of the Africans that laid it using their own tears as mortar to hold it in place even as they endured the hardships of chattel slavery. The pressures of undue pain created the rich unique Gullah/Geechee culture including its language that is so sought after by researchers and tourists. Often in their search to simply hear the language, taste the food, hear a tale told or a song sung, they do not pay attention to the priceless jewel that Gullah/Geechee actually is.

The Gullah/Geechee people have contributed a great deal to human history. Yet, there are few that are aware of their varied contributions. They are treated just as their ancestors were-relegated to being nameless or renamed. Numerous doctoral theses, books, and documentaries seek to now delve into the stories of what happened to Africans that were kidnapped and captured and ended up in North America and in particular, in "the South." Even as they uncover documents concerning these Africans that became enslaved and they write of their relation- ships to others such as the indigenous/Native Americans and other people of African descent whose roots in what was to be called "America" grew in the north, they do not call these folks Gullah/Geechees. They are simply relegated into the amalgamated term "African American" or relegated to having no humanity by continuing to be called "slaves."

As there are many attempts to reconstruct the occurrences that are shaping the choices and behaviors of people of African descent worldwide, the Gullah/Geechee people and who they truly are cannot be left out of that story nor can their beginning which came about in the pressure cooker that is now referred to as the "institution of chattel slavery" or the "TransAtlantic Slave Trade."

"Very early in the seventeenth century, when our great Eastern states were yet in the infancy of colonial life, our good mother England wanted to increase her North American colonial products for home consumption and for re-exportation; and she wanted, besides, to discourage the emigration of her European subjects to the new world, where they were disposed to seek refuge from the oppressions of the restoration. To accomplish these ends, she did not hesitate to violate the spirit of her own ancient common law, by fastening upon us the curse of the negro slavery. King Charles II, by public proclamation, called upon his loyal subjects to subscribe to a joint stock company organized under government auspices, for the declared purpose of 'importing African slaves into America." The stock was readily taken, and our Atlantic coasts became dumping grounds for the slaves." (Magazine of American History July 1892 Edited by Martha J. Lamb, NY, How England Forced the Slave Upon America p.34)

The kidnapping, capture, enslavement, importation, and sale of the "commodity" which was African people who became labeled "black gold" or "black cargo" was rapidly considered a way of life that had to be maintained in the area of "Chicora." "Chicora" was renamed Carolina (prior to it being split into North and South Carolina). Numerous families that originated in

England's names are throughout the state of South Carolina. They can still be seen on signs on roads and buildings. Thus, the mark of enslavement continues to last as even new institutions are built. These names echo out the history of what took place throughout the areas that began as colonies and are now called states in the United States of America.

Just as when one travels the terrain of the United States from state to state today, there are differences in cultures and in the way that the architecture, the environment, and key elements of the economies are dealt with to make up the larger "American economic base" which has its foundation on the backs of these enslaved Africans. The trade of Africans involved African skills and knowledge throughout. The capture and sale of the

Africans on the continent was the initial setting. Africans were next enslaved on many islands off the West Coast of Africa before they were loaded on to the ships of those traders that were looking for their particular type of cargo.

After a journey through the middle passage to the Caribbean or onward to the "New World," the artistry, scientific knowledge, and skills of the Africans were put to use to heal Africans that had become ill due to the journey. These Africans needed to appear as "good stock" for sale or they would not bring the highest dollar at an auction. They had tar rubbed on their skin to cover any cuts that had been inflicted by whips when Africans fought back or would not move on command. Once the Africans were sold and distributed onto plantations, they had to show what they knew in the fields, with herbology, with blacksmithing, etc. Some were even brought simply to be cooks or as breeders to have more children that would work for free or be fattened up and auction off as the "commodities" that they were considered to be.

Many of the Africans were required to work with ship building as well. Without the ships that were navigated to bring in the cargo or to take the items that they cultivated out to markets around the world, there would not have been a successful "slave trade." Due to continued greed and struggles for control, strife came amongst the English oppressors in England and those that had left that land to become "colonist" that were enslaving the Africans in the New World. "The navigation act, requiring all trading ships to be built either in England or her plantations, and to be manned by crews of who two thirds must be British subjects, was not a matter of complaint, for it ruled through the whole empire and was supposed to be everywhere beneficial. The commercial code very early enacted was a different affair, by the provisions of which the interests of the colonists were sacrificed to the selfishness and greediness of manufacturers and merchants at home, who had votes to use the sharply divided parliaments of that day. By the time the colonies had tobacco, cotton, silk, coffee, indigo, naval stores, skins, sugar, and rice to sell, they are forbidden to make a market outside of the British dominions. No goods could be carried from Europe to America without being first landed in England and reshipped. Every form of colonial industry that could possibly compete with the same manufacture in the mother country was deliberately crushed." (Lamb, Martha, Magazine of

American History August 1889, "England's Struggle with the American Colonies" p. 122-123)

The commercial codes were only the first blow that the colonists would feel hitting them and the pillars that held up the institution that they felt was needed to continue for the benefit of themselves and their future generations. On March 22, 1794, Congress passed an act prohibiting the African slave trade. Thus, another blow struck the pillars.

On March 2, 1807 they passed another supplemental act to take effect January 1, 1808. This was no doubt a choice that was made after the British had fought those that had "rebelled" against them during the American Revolution. The British knew that if this economic system of enslavement would not exist, the colonies could not sustain themselves.

Numerous colonists in Carolina were not about to accept orders from those that they felt were threatening their way of life in spite of the fact that their way of life was built on denying the human rights of the Africans. General Charles C. Pinckney (whose home in Mount Pleasant, South Carolina in the Gullah/Geechee Nation is now a National Historic Site that is owned and operated by the United States Department of the Interior's *National*

Park Service) stated: "As to the restriction upon the African trade after 1808, your delegates had to contend with the religious and political prejudices of the Eastern and Middle States, and the interested and inconsistent opinion of Virginia. So long as there is an acre of swamp-land uncultivated in South Carolina, I favor the importation of negroes. Our climate, and the flat, swampy situation of our country, obliges us to cultivate our lands with them. Without them, the State would be a desert." (Lamb p. 159)

If the truth were told, the state would still "be a desert" without the knowledge and the love of the land of Gullah/Geechee people. They have kept the land fertile and the waterways pristine even as areas north of them became polluted and damaged. The Gullah/Geechees had and continue to build the huge plantation houses and clubhouses of the very people that enslaved their ancestors and many that seem to be coming forth to re-enslave them to positions of servitude in gated resort and retirement areas. Enslavement during the 1600s, 1700s, and 1800s was fueled by the same energy that caused the displacement of Gullah/Geechees in mass during the 1900s-financial greed.

"But what goad is more potent than money, what passion more ruthless than the passion for it? If we accept that this is what society was like, it does not exonerate us from peering back into a peculiarly sunless and fungoid region of our proud island past."(Pope-Hennessy, James, Sins of the Fathers: A Study of the Atlantic Slave Traders 1441-1807 P. 5)

As pain filled as blatant facts are for many people, Gullah/Geechee people live each day looking at the past and living through it in a world of Sankofa. They continue to "go back an fetch it" on a daily basis. They know that "ef hunnuh ain kno whey hunnuh dey frum, hunnuh ain gwine kno whey hunnuh da gwine." So, the past is the present and the way that we act within it will determine our future.

In spite of the efforts of the local, state, and United States federal legislative bodies, the tourism agents and agencies, the misdirected educational institutions that are run by those that do not accept the grassroots knowledge of people that live a culture and pass their story on orally, or the destructioneers that build resorts and gated retirement areas on the sacred grounds of the

Gullah/Geechee Nation to re-enslave Gullah/ Geechees, Gullah/Geechee people seek to speak their own story replete with pain, horror, joy, and laughter. Most of all, it is a story of survival and strength. There have been repeated attempts to bury this strength, but even concrete sidewalks and paved roads cannot hide the voices that cry out from Cha'stun!

Sullivan's Island-
> The Entryway of Enslavement

"...slaves must be bought and sold; somebody must do the trading; and why not make hay while the sun shines?"

(Sins of the Fathers: A Study of the Atlantic Slave Traders 1441-1807 by James Pope-Hennessy, 1998 Barnes and Noble Inc. New York, NY p. 3)

If the doorway opening to the Atlantic Island at Goree in West Africa is seen as "the door of no return," the shoreline of Sullivan's Island can definitely be seen as the entryway to enslavement. According to Junius P. Rodriguez in the "Historical Encyclopedia of World Slavery:"

"Until the mid-fifteenth century, slavery had been practiced extensively in various cultures and settings, but it had never been affiliated with race or ethnicity. Enslavement was simply the custom that befell people who had been defeated in conflict and were captives of war. In a theoretical sense, it was a humanitarian gesture that prevented the wholesale execution of captives, but the notion began to change as European navigators explored the coastline of

West Africa and large-scale commerce in a human commodity began to develop." (Rodriguez, xviii)

Sullivan's Island which is north of the peninsula that is now the City of Charleston and east of the Town of Mount Pleasant served as a connection point that more Africans enslaved in America would share than any other. "From the founding of Charleston in 1670, blacks were imported into the region, first in small numbers from the West Indies and then in ever-greater numbers directly from Africa." (Pollitzer in Goodwine's Legacy of Ibo Landing 54)

An Act of 1707 called for the first "pest" or "pestilence" house or "lazaretto" on Sullivan's Island. As they came in from Africa or "Alkebulan," they were stopped off in these buildings at Sullivan's Island before they would ever get to the destination that they had been captured to arrive at-the auction block.

This island was appropriated to the state for defense and quarantine in 1787. By 1791 it had also ironically become a place that was a summer village that people came to escape getting malaria and to enjoy the beach front at such areas as "Moultrieville" which was outside of the fort there. The town was incorporated in 1817 and continues to be a location of beach villas that literally "overlook" the true story of the place.

"Sullivan's Island off Charleston Harbor has been styled the black man's Ellis Island since through it flowed more of the forced African immigration that settled the lower south than through any other single location in the eighteenth century. It was gateway to the most expansive plantation economy on the continent in the quarter century before the Revolution, an economy that drew equally from Africa and Europe the human material essential to claim the hinterland for cultivation." (SC Historical Magazine, "Charleston and Internal Slave Redistribution" by Daniel C Littlefield April 1986 p. 105) Although some have "styled" this as an "Ellis Island," they gave an incorrect moniker to this place of horror because Ellis Island served as a place of hope for those that chose to come to North America. No one would have chosen to see Sullivan's Island as their first point of arrival in a new land nor would they have chosen to come without personal effects (as people brought in trunks to Ellis

Island) nor in chains as did the Africans.

"The smallpox that hit Charleston in 1697 came from Virginia and reappeared several times thereafter. Although the disease could have been brought by whites, colonists became especially concerned about blacks as a source after the number of slaves directly from Africa increased. In fear of pestilence, in 1698 vessels were forbidden to pass a point one mile east of Sullivan's Island until the pilot had ascertained from the captain whether there was contagious disease aboard. A brick pest house was built on Sullivan's Island in 1707, and by 1712 a health officer was required to go aboard all ships to inquire about disease and the cause of any deaths." (Donnan, Documents Illustrative of the History of the Slave Trade to America, Vol. 4, p. 62)

One of the diseases that the Africans endured by making it across the Middle Passage was called "flux." This was actually a violent form of dysentery. If the enslaved continued to suffer from this condition at auction time, slave traders plugged the enslaved African's anus with cotton in order to have him or her appear healthy at auction.

"When a slave ship came in and stopped at Sullivan's Island to perform the mandatory ten days quarantine (or longer if the slaves possessed a contagious disease), a merchant or merchant company had to take charge of the cargo and arrange for its sale. In the meantime, the merchant had to have sufficient cash reserves for personal credit to be able to pay out of hand the ship captain's coast commission, the men's half-wages and other possible requisite charges. He conducted the sale on the best conditions possible-meaning at the best prices and on the short- est terms, ranging, generally, from three months to a year; but he was responsible for all bad debts.

Planters who could pay cash got a discount; the others paid interest ranging as high at 25% at the beginning of the century, but dropping 10% in 1720 and to 8% in 1748." (Littlefield, "Charleston and Internal Slave Redistribution" p.94)

"Henry Laurens, a leading slave merchant of Charleston, South Carolina, was thinking in these terms when he described the Negro trade in his colony to a Barbadian firm in 1756: 'tis much more difficult to run off these small parcells (sic) than Cargo of 3 or 400, when such a Number are for Sale it draws down the People from every part of the Province and one bids upon the other, very often they in their hurry take hold of very ordinary Slaves as prime, overlooking their imperfections which in a small parcell [n] ever escapes notice..."(Henry Laurens to Law, Satterthwaite, and Jones, Jan. 12, 1756, in Donnan Documents, Wax 12)

Although "minor damage to the imported goods" was often overlooked, especially if "doctored up" in the right way, the purchasers were very particular about where the cargo came from. In the beginning, colonists did not want Africans from Calabar in Charles Towne. However, they wanted Gambians and tall Africans. From 1735 to 1739 11,000 Africans came through Sullivan's Island. "The time of arrival is also significant. In the Early Period, 1716-44, three-fourths of the 22,117 Africans imported into Charleston came from Angola, a fact that explains their influence on later arrivals. In the great Middle Period, 1749-87, when 63,210 or half of all Africans arrived, Senegambia accounted for one-third, and the bulge of West Africa from Senegambia through the Bight of Biafra contributed more than three-fourths. In the Final Period, those four feverish years from 1804 through 1807-when 29,461 were brought into Charleston-Angolans were again in the majority." (Pollitzer in Goodwine 58)

"While slaving captains conducted the exchange with the natives, purchasing the recently captured Negroes, their vessels lay along the coast for long periods of time. There the master and crew were subject not only to diseases and the hardships of life in hot, humid Africa, but to attacks by blacks who were not enslaved. It was not uncommon for the Negroes to grow dissatisfied with the trading and to employ force. Perhaps they disliked the demands made by the whites, or believed that the goods offered in trade were of inferior quality. It may have been that some innocent slaving ship was merely being punished for the crimes committed by the vessel that had preceded it in that area.

A victim of one of these native attacks was said to have been 'cut-off.' Thus the South Carolina Gazette reported in 1759 (July 7, 1759) that

The Ship Polly, Capt. Hamilton, and the Ship Mercury, Capt. Ingledieu both of

Bristol, were lately lost on the Coast of Africa. Capt. Hamilton was destined for this Port [Charleston] with a Cargo of Slaves. A Sloop commanded by a Brother of the above Capt. Ingledieu, slaving up the River Gambia, was attacked by a Number of Natives, about the 27th of February last, and made a good Defence; but the Captain finding himself desperately wounded, and likely to be overcome, rather than fall into the Hands of such merciless Wretches, when about 80 Negroes had boarded his Vessel, discharged a Pistol into his Magazine, and blew her up; himself and every Soul on Board perished. The Skow Perfect, Capt. William Potter, of Liverpool, bound for this Port, is also cut off by the Negroes in the River Gambia and every Man on board murdered; and the vessel lost." (Donald D Wax, *Negro Resistance to the Early American Slave Trade, The Journal of Negro History Vol. LI*-January 1966-No.1 p.4-5)

The enforcement of the practice of "seasoning" was no doubt put in place as a result of the Africans continuing time and again to take back what was rightfully theirs-freedom! At places like Sullivan's Island, just as at the many places of enslave- ment along the coast of West Africa-Goree, James

Island, Bunce Island, etc-Africans were starved or given very little food to make them weak. Africans were beaten again and again in order to subdue their will to fight. This "seasoning" would often fade like someone adding water to a well seasoned pot and Africans would again battle once they arrived at the plantations to which they were distributed after the sale on the auction block. The auction block that was to hold the blood, sweat, and tears of the most Africans that were enslaved in the North America was that of Charles Town "doung de ribba frum Sullivan's Islandt."

Ef Ashlee Would Ta'k ta Wi

"If slavery as an economic system was inevitable in the mainland's southern colonies, the immigration of these Barbadian planters hastened its coming and consolidated its uses. Among those who moved to the mainland were scions of Barbados's richest families, who arrived with the means to set up successful new business concerns. These businesses blossomed, creating opportunities for immigrants who were equally ambitious but of lesser means. Through migration to the American mainland, Englishmen who would have remained small planters or struggling businessmen on the island found themselves elected to the state assembly and establishing dynasties of their own. They brought their families, their social habits, and their prejudices with them, and their stamp on the new colonial frontier was unmistakable."

(Burnside and Robotham, *Spirits of the Passage: The Transatlantic Slave Trade in the Seventeenth Century* p. 158)

The British Lord's Proprietors and the other British that would follow them to the New World and set up a plantation existence on these sacred lands brought their "families, their social habits, and their prejudices with them" to the home of many indigenous Americans that had dwelled on this land for thousands of years. Although many documents will state that the Etiwan Indians lived on the Cooper River and the Wando Indians lived on Wando River until 1675, South Carolina Historical Magazine's "Renaming Charleston Rivers" (p. 42 & 43 January 1988 Chas, SC) states that "the Indians did not consider the portion of the river that runs along the north side of the Charleston peninsula to be part of the present Cooper River. As a consequence, when European names were eventually assigned to replace Indian names, there was uncertainty for decades about what the new names applied to.

When the settlers started sending letters to the proprietors, they put 'kiawah' as their return address. Sandford's report of his discoveries had not been published, and the settlers were unaware that Sandford had named the Kiawah. Writing back in a lordly manner, Ashley Cooper informed the settlers, '...that you may not hereafter mistake the name of the place you are in, you are to take notice that the River was by Captain Sandford long since named Ashley River, and is still to be soe' [sic] This took care of the naming of the Ashley, but left the other rivers without European names."

"There is no doubt that the Etiwan Indians lived primarily on the upper Cooper River, but they claimed land as far down as the Charleston peninsula on the west side of the Cooper River and as far down as Daniel's Island on the east side. Daniel's Island had been called Etiwan Island before it was twice renamed."

Lords Proprietors Plantation at Old Town Creek came into being during 1699 as a plantation. After the Civil War, it was divided into small parcels of land. This place no longer can be detected in landscape nor name.

The continual renaming of the area continues to this day with the overtaking of parcels of land by new comers that want to gate areas off and rename historic areas to suit fantasies of plantation life "a la Gone With the Wind" instead of based on the history of the actual plantations that made up this land now called "Charleston." After the removal of the indigenous Americans that dwelled here, the names of the land masses have changed, the spellings of names that remain have changed as well. Some of the names that now adorn signs to gated areas, schools, teams, stores, etc. are Kiawah which was once spelled, "Keywah" which meant "where we now live." This was also the name given to the river that is now called the "Ashley River." Kiawah were noted to have dwelled on what is now called "Bull's Island."

"Sewee" at Sewee Harbor changed to "Bull's Bay." Sewee occupied the Mount Pleasant area also. The area took on the current name after James Hibben bought the Jacob Motte's estate in 1803 and named it for its 20 ft "high bluff."

These indigenous Americans along with the Edista or Edisto and the Sanpa, San, or Sanpit and Westoe lived along the Ashley and other rivers around the area. According to "South Carolina Indians, Indian Traders, and Other Ethnic Connections Beginning in 1670" (1998 Teresa M. Hicks Spartanburg, SC Reprint Company Publishers), Etiwan occupied what is now the city of Charleston. By 1680 Sewee, Wando, and Sampa lived in 3 separate settlements within 5 miles of each other on both sides of the Wando [Cooper] River. Sewee, Wando and Sampa had separate settlements along the Cooper River.

Sewee were in Christ Church Parish between Wando [Cooper] River, Awendaw Creek, and the Atlantic Ocean.

In 1708, 1/3 of the enslaved were Native American. Westo and Winia Indians were largely among that group. They usually did not include adult males because they were often killed and burned. Many indigenous Americans were enslaved for sale in the West Indies.

About 1721-1728 a large amount of the Edisto moved in with the Kiawah. The Edistos moved from the Port Royal/St. Helena Island area to Edisto Island.

The Kiawahs helped with the wars against the Yemassees. Yamassees and Tuscaroras and Creeks and Cherokees would assist one another. As they battled each other, the battle with the Europeans that were coming into their homeland began to increase. The river ways and the lands as they had known them were about to have drastic changes take place.

King Charles II gave the Lords Proprietors a charter covering what are now North Carolina, South Carolina, Georgia, and west- ward. William Sayle led the expedition to colonize Carolina. After stopping at Port Royal for a couple days, they went to Albemarle Point on the Ashley River that was then "Kiawah" just as the Cooper River was then "Etiwan." Near this or a part of this was also written to have been the "Weepoolow River." Lord Shaftesbury, who was the chief of the Proprietors, renamed these rivers. In April 1670, the first settlement of English colonists was on the west bank of the Ashley River, which they called "the Kiawah." They then renamed the site for George Monck who was one of the Lords Proprietors. November 1, 1670 Lord Ashley wrote to Gov. Joseph West directing that the new town should be called "Charles Town" for his benefactor, King Charles II.

Old Towne Plantation was part of where the settlement across the river called "Oyster Point" which is now "Charles Towne Landing State Historic Site" between the Ashley and Wando (Cooper) Rivers. This was the first permanent settlement in South Carolina. It was founded in 1670 and in 1680 the land was abandoned. When the Lords Proprietors settled Oyster Point Town between the rivers and in 1679 public records were brought there. It began to be called "New Charles-town" and by 1682 as "Charles-Town." The name became Charleston when it was incorporated in

1783. Charleston was the capital of South Carolina until 1786 when Columbia was legislated into existence.

On the 20th of December 1671 a group of new arrivals were sent to found a branch settlement called James Towne on James Island at New Town Creek as well. James Island would eventually be divided into a number of plantations just as all along the Ashley River would. Drayton Hall, which started to be built in 1738 and was not completed for four years, admits that it was built by the Africans that were brought in and enslaved there.

Middleton Place and Drayton Hall Plantations have become some of the major tourist sites for visitors to Charleston, SC. Drayton Hall Plantation was named for John Drayton who began the building of the house that is currently there in 1738. It was completed in 1742.

In 1974 the house was acquired by the *National Trust for Historic Preservation* and is open to the public. When the Drayton family sold the property to the *National Trust* in 1974, they sold 633 acres. Today the *National Trust* holds 125 acres, and the State of South Carolina holds the remainder of this former indigo and rice plantation.

Magnolia Plantation was called "Magnolia on the Ashley" and is now open to the public. It began as the land grant of Maurice Matthews in 1677, but in 1680 John Drayton built a home there. This house was destroyed by the Union in 1865 during the Civil War. This was the end of what had been a rice plantation that enslaved at least 300 Africans.

Vaucluse Plantation sat on the Southeast side of Drayton Hall Plantation. It was formed in 1678 and named after a town in France by Jonathan Fitch. Thomas Middleton built a house on the 1100 acres and lived there until his death.

Middleton Place is along the Ashley with Drayton Hall. This was the home of Henry Middleton, who was born in England, but became a member of the First Continental Congress. It grew to be a major rice plantation. At one point, Middleton owned 50,000 acres of land that was split into 20 different plantations.

Wraggs Plantation is upriver from Middleton Place. It has been called "Smith-Wragg," and "St Giles" over the years due to ownership by William

Loughton Smith who married Charlotte Wragg in 1805, William Wragg Smith, and Samuel Wragg. 1875 the plantation was sold and the majority of the 4300 acres was purchased by a paper company.

Uxbridge Plantation was also owned by Johnson William Wragg. In 1766, he sold a portion of it which became "Salt Hill Plantation" and another parcel that became known as "Uxbridge."

The Runnymede Plantation in Ladson is on the West bank of the Ashley River. This plantation has also been called "Green- ville," "Runimede," and "Sarah Place." In 1705 the plantation was granted to John Cattell. However, it was not until William Bull Pringle came along that a mansion was built on the 1,457 acres. Pringle's mansion was destroyed by the Union Army in 1865. Charles Cotesworth Pinckney obtained the property during the 1930s and built the mansion on the property.

Stephen Bull of Kingshurst Hall in Warwickshire, England was the father of Stephen Bull who immigrated in on the ship *Carolina* to Charles Town in 1670. He was part of gentry. Bull dealt in Indian and African trade. Indian traders would normally have creditors that would be based many times in

London. It would provide goods to colonial merchants in Charles Town.

"Ashley Hall Plantation" was named for Anthony Ashley Cooper who was one of the British Lords Proprietors. In 1676 it came into existence as a plantation. By 1704 Stephen Bull, who had been granted the land, was living here with his children. His oldest son built a large plantation house which Colonel William Izard Bull set fire to it. He did not want the Union to occupy it, so he set it ablaze amidst the 1000 acres surrounding it.

There is also "Ashley Hill Plantation" which was also called "Batavia." This location south of Middleton Place was formed in 1732.

When Bull died he was buried at Ashley Hall Plantation. He left six enslaved Africans and 1,000 acres of land to his heirs. The Bulls married Draytons and Middletons. "Middleton Place and Marshlands and Boone Hall [which is a tourist attraction located in the Mount Pleasant area and is toured by thousands and filmed each year) owe their existence to hard bargaining for human flesh in the Gambia or Benin." (Pope-Hennessy p. 225)

All along the banks of the Ashley River

these places of hardship and human bondage are now called "gardens" and "plantation gardens." Highway 61 takes visitors to the West Ashley area by the thousands year after year. They visit sites that have been redesigned to mask the reality of the brutality to which they owe their foundation and existence.

Further down the river is Pierpont Plantation which was named for Benjamin Pierpont. This is a Revolutionary War battle site at which an earthen fort was built. About 1780 or 1781, Sir Henry Clinton, the British commander, and a company of Hessians, a company of German soldiers known as the Green Coats, fought at this location. The 824 acre property was divided into the "Pierpont on the Ashley," subdivision by the Pierpont Corporation in 1933. However, George Bedon or Beadon received a grant for 510 acres at the location in 1677. He built a plantation house that was burned by Union soldiers in 1865.

Over the years the property has had several owners and numerous uses. During from the 1940s to 1960 Ferdinanda "Ferdie" Legare Waring operated "Old Town Gardens," from which she sold flowers for commercial florists and marketed eggs.

By 1699, the 338 acre "Millbrook" or "Jackson Plantation" sat further down on the South side of the Ashley River. This land was granted to James Humpreys.

North of Stony Point on the East Bank of the Ashley River, Thomas Rose received a land grant in 1677. He formed a plantation at that site.

The "Farmfield Plantation" is now a housing subdivision. However, in 1854 William Ravenel built a house there that was placed on the *National Register of Historic Places* in 1854. It was one of the few houses in Saint Andrews Parish to survive the Civil War. This 250 acre rice plantation continued to be operated as a farm by the Ravenels until 1920. After that the property began to change hands.

"Orange Grove" or the "Accabee Plantation" on the Eastern bank of the Ashley River was formed during 1713 as a colonial plantation. It passed through the hands of the Elliott, Morris, Rose and Edward C. Perroneau families over the years. "Grove" or "Grove Farm" was started in 1701. The first house burned down and the present one was built in 1786 by John Abbott

Hall. He had 328 acres instead of the 14 acres where the house sits.

Gullah/Geechees throughout Charleston trace their ancestry to these plantations in what is now called "West Ashley." Some begin their trace on the peninsula to "Aiken-Rhett" or "Lowndes Grove Plantation" which is now a bed and breakfast at 260 St Margaret Street near The Citadel and Hampton Park.

"The phenomenal growth of colonial Charleston from an isolated hideaway on the Ashley River in 1670 to become, within a few decades, the major transoceanic port in the New World was due, in large measure, to its strategic location on the principal trade routes of the times as they crossed back and forth over the North Atlantic. These trade routes actually followed the pathways of a massive clockwise-rotating system of winds and wind-driven currents which literally pushed and ferried the relatively small and unwieldy square-rigged sailing ships of the colonial period around an eight-thousand-mile elliptical track interconnecting the North Atlantic coastlines of Europe, Africa, and North America.

***Charleston was located just over

halfway around this elliptical tract at a point where the northeast-flowing ocean currents reach their maximum volumes. In effect, Charleston was positioned at the southwest terminus of an axis which followed the most direct and fastest sailing route of the times between the midatlantic [sic] colonial ports and the European ports far to the northeast. As a result of these natural advantages, together with the productivity of its agrarian economy, Charles- ton soon became not only the third largest port in the colonies, in terms of total trade, but it became the major colonial port in terms of direct transatlantic commerce, a position it maintained for as long as square-rigged sailing ships of the colonial period of imperial expansion were relied upon as the principal vehicles of marine transportation." (Pine "History Rides the Winds to Colonial Charleston" p. 162-163) In the 1750s the ship building centers were Charleston, Beaufort, and Georgetown with major building locations at Wando and Hobcaw.

In addition to commerce by water, commerce by land was on-going between the coastal area which is now called "the Lowcountry" and the inland part of the state. "A bustling though limited commerce operated between the two sections. From the beginning, deerskins were an important Back Country export to Charleston. The Camden area also became an important source of flour for the Low Country. Cattle drives to Charleston were annually staged from the Peedee, the upper Santee, and other grazing centers. Quantities of indigo, tobacco, hemp, and corn were sent to Charleston. In return Charleston merchants supplied the Back County with manufactured goods and other necessities." (Brown, "The South Carolina Regulators" p. 16)

"Charleston, SC, had important advantages as a port that helped it to become one of the South's leading exporters of lumber in the antebellum period. With a good harbor, extensive trade lines with the interior guaranteed by South Carolina's numerous rivers, a population of men of substance and energy, and, at its founding, the closest proximity of the English settlements to the West Indies, Charleston was destined to become an important lumber center." (Eisterhold, "Charleston: Lumber and Trade in a Declining Southern Port". p.61)

"The exploitation of South Carolina's timber resources was seriously under way well before the end of the colonial period. Charlestonians, hoping to make fortunes from cutting timber and lumber for the export trade, began occupying the lands bordering the Santee River within a few years after the founding of Charleston." (Eisterhold, p. 61)

"Like other South Atlantic communities, Charleston was handicapped by the westward migration of many of her more able skilled white artisans. This shortage of white labor forced lumbermen in Charleston, other communities, and in the interior to employ skilled slaves and free Negroes. Slaves working in Charleston mills, yards, and allied businesses outnumbered free Negroes and white employed in the same operations by 1848. Opinions varied on the quality of slave labor. One disgusted mill owner offered to sell a Negro sawyer because of the slave's weakness for liquor. Another Charleston lumberman offered employment to any sawyer if he could prove 'honesty, sobriety, industry, and knowledge of the business.' Not all skilled Negroes, however, were so poorly regarded. One was sold in 1837 at private sale in Charleston who had had 15 years' experience as an engineer and sawyer in steam sawmills and was described as a valuable employee. Generally, however, mill and yard owners preferred to utilize Negro labor in unskilled or semi-skilled positions, as stackers, wagoners, or in other similar positions. In 1851, for example, the Charleston Steam Saw Mill hired 20 Negroes to fill such positions. Thousands of other free Negroes and slaves found permanent or temporary employment as axemen, raftsmen, or in other capacities connected with lumbering the interior."

"Factors" were commission merchants that not only marketed rice and were the location to purchase plantation supplies, but also acted as the banker for the plantation owners. He would carry the plantation owners balance on deposit and used it to cover drafts as needs arose. He brought bills of exchange, gave

advise on investments, went to the market to purchase all forms of property from bank and railroad stock to plantations and even voted at stockholders meetings. The factor's most important job was selling the crops, but these crops could not be produced without the skills of the enslaved. Thus, the factors would also broker those with trades.

"Most of the highly skilled positions

in Charleston sawmills and lumberyards were held by whites. Considerable opposition existed among white artisans to the hiring of slaves and free Negroes in the trades in Charleston, and this was also true in other cities of the Old South." (Eisterhold p. 64-65)

Gibbs, Williams, and Company "sought to increase efficiency and profits by the erection of its own steam sawmill in November of 1837. Employing approximately 20 people, mostly Negro, this company survived the Panic of 1837 and operated their mill for about ten years before dissolving the company. Located on the corner of Council and Tradd Streets, the company had a large wharf from which vessels could load lumber for coastal and international markets, and apparently also did some business with the New York Steam Packet Company during the 1840's." (Eisterhold p. 67)

"Largely because of the volume of lumber brought into Charles- ton, the Santee Canal was one of the busiest and most profitable of the Southern canals, regularly paying dividends to its stockholders. Some lumber was also brought into the Charleston market on the cars of the Southern Carolina

Railroad and of the Charleston and South Carolina Railroad." (Eisterhold, p. 68)

"Another prominent Charleston factor and yard owner was John Dougherty, who in the 1850s bought and consigned lumber and timber for West Indian and European markets. Dougherty specialized in the purchase of shipping timber, which he obtained regularly by contracting with lumbermen in the interior...Like most factors, Dougherty stocked only the most reliable lumber products, articles for which there was a stable continuing demand in the West Indies. Cypress and oak shingles were always in much demand in the islands to over the roofs of planters and businessmen. On the island of St. Kitts in the East Caribbean, for example, several of the eighteenth and nineteenth century homes still standing and occupied today bear their original cypress shingled roofs, most of the shingles having been obtained from Southern factors like Dougherty." (Eisterhold p. 69) Other factors in the area were George Oleny, J H Maay, and T B Trout to name a few.

"Though its stratus-conscious residents looked down upon most occupations other than that of planter, factoring was considered a worthy occupation in antebellum Charleston. Charleston factors traded lumber and other products to the West Indies for slaves, sugar, liquor, and other goods, and this trade in the eighteenth century brought in specie to Charleston (and to the South) at a time when an unfavorable balance of trade with England was draining hard money from the American colonies. By the turn of the century, a number of prominent Charlestonians listed their occupations as 'lumber merchants'.

The West Indian carrying trade was the backbone of Charleston's lumber trade for much of the colonial and antebellum period. St. Croix was one of the islands with which South Carolina lumber factors developed lasting commercial arrangements. While trade had existed between Charleston and the island during the colonial period, commerce continued and intensified during the first half of the nineteenth century. St. Croix sugar, and extracts of sugar as well as European luxuries brought into St. Croix, were often reshipped to Charleston and sold by Charleston merchants, like George Gibbons and Company, wholesale from their large warehouses in exchange for lumber sent to St. Croix. John Tyler was another Charleston lumber factor who also ran a large store, bringing St. Croix products into Charleston. In turn, St. Croix merchants in Frederiksted and Christiansted, who sold or consigned sugar and other products to American vessels coming into their ports, stocked South Carolina (and other American) lumber in their yards. Findlay and Company of Frederiksted sent large quantities of West Indian sugar and rum to South Carolina ports, while buying large shipments of pine lumber, laths, staves, and cypress shingles for their yard from the same vessels. Findlay and Company then sold the lumber on the island, or reshipped it to neighboring islands, like St. Thomas." (Eisterhold p. 70)

The "decline in Charleston's importance as a lumber port can be observed in her trade relations with England during the period. British and other foreign ships frequently loaded with lumber in American ports in order to bring back full and saleable cargoes if enough rice or cotton was not available in Charleston, or if the price demanded for them was not acceptable...[John] Bunch [the British Consul for North Carolina] bitterly complained two years later about the unjust policy on the part of Charleston city officials of locking up colored English seamen who were unfairly regarded as potential incendiaries by the people." (Eisterhold p. 72)

"Although serious disagreements between the two sections persisted, the presence of South Carolina's huge slave population forestalled serious conflict. From 1730 to 1770 'the danger of insurrection by the new and half-savage slaves...remained perhaps the strongest influence in the province on public policy; and the interior settlements played an important role in dealing with that peril.

During the eighteenth century the Negro population of the Low Country increased by leaps and bounds until the whites were outnumbered at least two to one. Aside from the threat of an uprising, the planters lived under the constant anxiety that more and more Negroes might escape to the frontier to live with the Indians and make common cause with them against the whites. The predominantly white population of the Back Country was viewed as a counterpoise against the 'internal enemy,' the slaves. The Low Country was well aware that a large-scale black rebellion would probably swamp it unless the Back Country came to its assistance. The assurance that the interior settlers would fight, almost to the last man, to put down a Negro revolt was a great comfort to the planters...

The existence of slavery was thus a powerful common interest that held the sections together." (Brown p. 17-18)

Edward and Arthur Middleton who were Barbadian merchants arrived in Carolina in late 1670s and settled 1700 acres in Goose Creek just north of Charleston. Within two years Edward had obtained 4130 acres in land grants. Arthur was Edward's son who built "The Oaks" (which was Sara and Edward's plantation) into a 5,000 acre plantation. He eventually represented Berkeley County in the Commons House of Assembly.

Arthur Middleton became the acting governor of South Carolina and he complained that the Spanish were receiving and harboring runaways. He felt that they were sending them back to rob and plunder them along with Indians that would kill the white people and carry off the enslaved.

While the group that would come to be the Anglo-Carolinians were bound together through their quest to keep the Africans enslaved, the Africans were bound together by bloodline, heritage, traditions, and homeland. They would also soon come to be bound together by the culture and language that they created as a means to protect themselves within these hostile conditions of enslavement. This unique language and culture that would both become known as Gullah/Geechee culture could not be swept away by the tide of exploitation nor that of the Ashley River along whose banks roots of Africa began to rise through the soil of North America.

Charleston:
The Cornerstone of the Black Gold Commodity Exchange

Of all the cities along the eastern seaboard and Gulf Coast of North America, Charleston, South Carolina and New York City were the major economic centers that built the infrastructure for the rest of all of what has come to be known as "The United States of America." As the cornerstones of enslavement were laid, the building blocks were then structured and laid by and through the blood, sweat, tears, and labor of the Africans that were entered this land in bondage. "The focal point of this forced African immigration was the port of Charleston...Charleston became the entrepôt of the overseas trade with Africa and elsewhere as well as the center of government and social life. As the colony's commercial center, Charleston was guaranteed a practical monopoly on the slave trade-a preeminence that extended, indeed, practically all the region between the Chesapeake and St. Augustine. In nearly all that area, planters came or sent to Charleston for their slaves." (Littlefield p. 93)

"The trade was carried on by British and South Carolina merchants, and the slave vessels, largely from New England, usually came consigned to a merchant who conducted a general importing trade in Charles Town. The arrival of cargo brought planters to the sale in great numbers. Henry Laurens, one of the leading slave importers in the province, mentioned a sale in 1755 attended forty or fifty planters from so great a distance as seventy miles from Charles Town.

The price of slaves depended in general upon the economic conditions of the province, although other factors contributed to the general fluctuation of prices which characterized the pre-revolutionary slave market. In 1756 Laurens wrote: 'The price of Slaves here while they are imported in moderate numbers is wholly influenced by the values of our Staples, Rice and Indigo, and these have been depreciated much below the prices of last Year, so have the Planters slacked in the purchase of Slaves, lowered the prices and lengthened out the Credit.' The price of slaves was so unstable that it is seldom remained the same for many months during the year." (Johnson p. 31)

"Henry Laurens was a partner in the firm of Austin and Laurens, which aimed to sell not more than seven hundred Negro slaves a year. There were some dozen firms handling the retail slave trade in Charleston, but in the mid-eighteenth century, Austin and Laurens were the largest and most successful of them all, with one quarter of the whole of Charleston trade in their hands...

He [Laurens] dealt in rice and indigo, rum, beer, wine and deerskins. On most of his goods he charged a five per cent commission, but for slaves, he raised this to ten." (Pope-Hennessy p.223) This was no doubt why he wrote a great deal concerning the fluctuation in the prices that were being obtained for this "commodity" that was often called "black gold" or "black cargo."

Many tend to believe that the only area that was an active part of the enslavement of Africans was in the southeastern United States. However, this network spanned the entire east coast. "Although the Newport [New England] slave merchants used Barbados as a main information centre on current prices, and also sold in other West Indian islands, they did a brisk, direct trade with Charleston firms, and almost regarded the city of Charleston as yet another West Indian island. Samuel William Vernon, of Newport, traded chiefly with Austin and Laurens..." (Pope-Hennessy p.237)

Hobcaw where Wando and Cooper join was a cluster of shipyards where ships were built. Many were built by the hands of African people. As the cargoes of Africans came in, the wealth of their knowledge went out aboard these on a consistent basis from the port of Charleston. This port linked the world together as capital held in Britain underwrote Charleston trade. Numerous names that are found on street signs and buildings in Charleston, London, and Liverpool today are those of such financiers of and those made wealthy by this on-going system of human cargo coming in and other commodities going out. Richard Maitland and other captains in the London-Charleston trade no doubt saw their fair share of profit from this. That profit by no means skipped the islands along their routes.

"Altogether, in most years during the eighteenth century, about a fourth to a third of the total tonnage entering Charleston came from or via the West Indies, while between 15 percent to 25 percent of the ships cleared from Charleston traded to the West Indies. This disparity can be partly explained by contemporary shipping routes. Prevailing wind patterns dictated that many

vessels from Britain came via the West Indies, while return ships entered Charleston from the West Indies then returned, by the 1760s, nearly forty ships based in the West Indies annually cleared the port of Charleston with return cargoes of rice and other commodities for Jamaica, Barbados, the Leeward Islands, and the Bahamas." (Greene p. 200-201)

The foundation of this trade system in human cargo and agricultural commodities created an aristocracy from the center of Charleston. "Per capita wealth in the Charleston District of South Carolina in 1774 was an astonishing £2,337.7 more than four times that of people living in the tobacco areas of the Chesapeake and nearly six times greater than that of people living in the towns of New York and Philadelphia.

Most wealthy rice planters chose Charleston as the site for their most elegant residence, and, with a library company, concerts, theatre, horse races, and a variety of benevolent organizations, fraternal groups, and social clubs. By 1770s, some South Carolina families had become so sufficiently wealthy that they were even following the example of West Indians and abandoning the colony altogether. In the early 1770s, as many as fifty absentee South Carolina proprietors were living in London." (Greene p. 207)

"Some of Charleston's slaveholding compounds were so large they might appropriately be called plantations. Many of the city's wealthy merchants kept more than twenty slaves in their house- holds. In some cases up to fifty people were crowded into dormitories behind their owner's house. While such a barracks-like slave quarters strongly resembled plantation housing in wide use in the Caribbean, the layout of other Charleston properties closely followed the pattern seen on plantations in the surrounding low country. At the Ward house on East Bay Street, for example, two large brick buildings intend to shelter both slaves and their labor mark a wide yard behind the main house and are much like the flanking dependencies found at the nearby Middleton and Drayton Hall plantations just up the Ashley River. Indeed, the arrangement at the Ward house replicates the usual geometry of a rural big house and its adjacent buildings and grounds.

The Robinson-Aiken house provides an even more vivid instance of a plantation arrangement in an urban setting." (Before Freedom Came 44-45) This home has become a historic site that host a number of sophisticated functions with no focus on how this building nor the peninsula that it sits on came to be nor whose shoulders it was built on.

Many that now come to live in Charleston and other parts of the Gullah/Geechee Nation today still carry on the business of being "absentees" in that they purchase homes on this wealthy peninsula which is now the historic City of Charleston and they live in the area only part time. Many of the people that dwell in Charleston and other parts of the Gullah/Geechee Nation also parallel the behavior of Laurens in that there is no concern for the welfare of the African people dwelling there. The concern is focused on personal gain and economic advancement with little or no concern about what is happening to other human beings. Laurens wrote extremely contradictory remarks regarding the "business" that he was in. In one document he wrote:

"I abhor Slavery...the day I hope is approaching when from principles of gratitude as well as justice every Man will strive to be foremost in shewing his readiness to comply with the golden Rule; not less than £20,000 sterling...would all my Negroes produce if sold a public Auction tomorrow, I am not the Man who enslaved them, they are indebted to English Men for that favour, nevertheless I am devising means for manumitting many of them & cutting off the entail of Slavery-great powers oppose me, the Laws & Customs of my Country, my own & the avarice of my Country Men-What will my Children say if I deprive them of so much Estate? These are difficulties but not insuperable I will do as much as I can in my time & leave the rest to a better hand." (Rogers p.273)

Laurens focused on leaving an inheritance to his children at all cost. The price that was paid was done in human flesh and blood. In order to keep the price up for such, he and others in the slave trade business sought methods by which to get and keep the price on Africans at a premium. "Late in the decade a strong black was priced at more than a thousand dollars- a price too high for large as well as small planters. 'Fresh Africans' would sell for no more than five hundred dollars each, and their introduction in large numbers would force down labor costs. The small planter, especially, was quick to sense the advantage in this scheme." (Williams p. 24)

"As early as 1794 Congress prohibited the trade to the United States by foreign carriers, and after 1808 the trade was made illegal, regardless of carrier. The Treaty of Ghent in 1815 and the Webster-Ashburton Treaty of 1842 provided for cooperation between United States and British navies to enforce the laws of both nations relative to the trade." (The Proceedings of The South Carolina Historical Association (c) 1960 Columbia, SC "The Southern Movement to Reopen the African Slave Trade, 1854-1860: A Factor in Secession" by Jack K Williams p. 23) The latter two treaties were not easily accepted by those who had built their entire lives on the foundation that African enslavement had been poured.

As debates began, representation on

both sides of the issue began to form. "South Carolina also provided the trade adherents with a leader, one Leonidas W Spratt, Charleston lawyer and editor. Not a plantation owner, his leadership seems to have stemmed from his belief that with the African trade the South in general and the city of Charleston in particular might regain lost prosperity." (The Proceedings of The South Carolina Historical Association (c) 1960 Columbia, SC "The Southern Movement to Reopen the African Slave Trade, 1854-1860: A Factor in Secession" by Jack K Williams p. 24) This lost prosperity had no doubt come through their battles for their own "freedom" from British rule. Yet, the freedom of the Anglo-Carolinians was based on the enslavement of the Africans. Therefore, they sent representatives to gather and make their position known.

"Ten states sent representatives to Montgomery." [1858]...and Spratt came forward with the following:

1. Slavery is right, and, being right, there can be no wrong in the natural means to its formation.

2. It is expedient and proper that the Foreign Slave Trade shall be reopened,

and this Convention will lend its influence to any legitimate means to that end.

3. A committee consisting of one from each Slave State shall be appointed to consider of the means consistent with the duty and obligations of these states for reopening the Foreign Slave Trade, and that they report their plan to the next meeting of this Convention."

(The Proceedings of The South Carolina Historical Association 1960 Columbia, SC "The Southern Movement to Reopen the African Slave Trade, 1854-1860: A Factor in Secession" by Jack K Williams p. 26)

"The fate of Charleston, Spratt warned, would be that of all the South, were slave trade laws allowed to remain in force. The 'splendors of Charleston had waned' as the importation of slaves decreased. Progress had left the city; the swamps had returned. Acres that once sold for fifty dollars now went for five. 'Once the Metropolis of America,' the great city was now the 'unconsidered seaport of a tributary province'."(Williams p. 27-28)

"Such was the state of things when telegraph keys ticked out the message that Lincoln had been elected President. As suddenly as it had drawn life in 1854 the agitation for a reopened trade expired. Secession was now the issue and all else was secondary." (Williams p. 31)

Pun De Plantayshun

Secession would leave its marks upon the lands that had all been plantations in Charleston. Many are now recognized as historic sites while others are built and walked upon daily without acknowledgement of what was there before.

"Encampment Plantation" Off Parkers Ferry Road near Jacksonboro Was once a military encampment. Prior to that it was "Sheppard Tract." This was no doubt during 1850 when it was a 950 acre cotton plantation. Oak Lawn Plantation in Parkers Ferry was also called "Pon Pon" where sea island cotton and rice were grown.

The 2,000 acre Haulover Plantation on Seabrook Island was half of the island which is bounded by Haulover Creek, Kiawah River, and the Atlantic Ocean. Rabbit Point Plantation was the other 2,000 acres of Seabrook Island. The plantation is now a gated area just as its neighbor that still bears the name of its original stewards-"Kiawah."

Kyawah, Kyawha, Oristo or "Kiawah Plantation" was located on the whole of Kiawah Island and bounded by the Kiawah River, the Stono River, and the

Atlantic Ocean. Kiawah Plantation, Kiawah Island, and today's Kiawah River (which separates Kiawah Island from Johns Island) are all named for a Cusabo tribe that lived on the western shore of what is now called the Ashley River. It became a 5,000 acre indigo plantation that enslaved 150 people in order to harvest the crops. A freedman named Quash was a vital part of the detailing of history of this place. "Your Servant, Quash: Letters of a South Carolina Freedman by the Chicora Foundation gives the following account:

Kiawah Island's English history begins with its "purchase" from the Kiawah Indians on March 10, 1675. The cost, "cloth, hatchets, beads & other goods and manufacturers," gave no hint of what the island would become in the twentieth century. The land, described as a 2700 acre plantation, was granted to Captain George Raynor by the Lords Proprietors on March 29, 1699. Some suggest that Raynor was a reformed pirate, welcomed in South Carolina because of his wealth. Regardless, he divided Kiawah, selling half to a Captain William Davis about a year after its purchase. The other half was passed to Raynor's daughter, Mary Raynor Moore.

By 1737 these two tracts of Kiawah were again united under one owner, John Stanyarne, a wealthy planter who lived on nearby John's Island and used his Kiawah plantation for cattle ranching and indigo production. When Stanyarne died in 1772, slavery was well established on Kiawah. In fact, Stanyarne owned 296 African-American slaves on his eight plantations and at his Charleston townhouse. His estate was valued at £146,246.9.2 – or about $2.5 million dollars.

Stanyarne's will passed the western half of Kiawah, including his settlement, to his grand daughter, Mary Gibbes. The eastern half of Kiawah Island was devised to his other grand daughter, Elizabeth Vanderhorst. This division of Kiawah into two plantations would last until the early twentieth century – and it also serves as the back drop for the history of Quash Stevens.

The first Vanderhorst's on Kiawah, Arnoldus Vanderhorst II and his wife Elizabeth built a plantation house and had upwards of 30 slaves tending cattle, growing subsistence crops like corn and peas, and planting indigo. This plantation was destroyed by the British in 1780, during the American

Revolution. By about 1785 Arnoldus Vanderhorst was again planting Kiawah with 40 slaves, although his new plantation house (still standing on Kiawah today) was not begun until about 1801. At that time a letter from the plantation's white overseer talking of being "obliged to flog several of the [African-American] carpenters" to keep them working.

During the first quarter of the nineteenth century Vanderhorst expanded his efforts on Kiawah, beginning to plant cotton. The number of slaves increased to 113 in 1810. But conditions were far from good and an 1801 letter remarks:

We have had a distressing time for this 8 or 10 days past With Sick negroes. chem is dead and Isac is very sick with apluricey. I was oblige to blister him this morning. big feby Has been very ill but is something better – I would send Isac down but it will not do to remove him in such weather. I first gave him a dose of salt and tartar and when his tongue was yet foul I gave him a second dose of hip and gallah. Gabo gave him spirits of turpentine with sweet oyl and also a sirup made of hour hound life everlasting alder and gave him. As it an ecelent remedy for the cold on the stomach. peter's got better, but Cupit is laid up. it is distressing to See So much sickness, and many worker calls about.

Toward the end of his life, Arnoldus manumitted seven slaves: Hagar Richardson and her three children, Sarah, Eliza, and Peter, as well as three additional slaves, Stepney, Molley, and Peter. Money was set aside to care for Hagar and her children and one of Hagar's children, Peter, legally took the Vanderhorst name upon reaching the age of 28. There is some evidence that at least Peter was a mulatto son of Arnoldus.

Upon Arnoldus' death in 1815, Kiawah was passed to his son, Elias Vanderhorst, who in 1821 married Ann Morris. Elias and Ann divided their time between Kiawah, their Charleston townhouse, and a summer retreat on Sullivan's Island. By 1830 they were also spending time at a house on Edisto Island's Eddings Bay.

Letters from the 1840s and 1850s present Kiawah as a rather forlorn island that produced few subsistence crops and even less cotton. Elias wrote in one letter that, "everything goes wrong here - no less than four prime hands [slaves] in the houses for life - two with snake bites, one with dropsy and the other with chronic sore throat." Later he would write that Kiawah "must be considered the Botany Bay," a reference to the Australian penal colony that the British government abandoned as unlivable. This may explain why the number of Kiawah slaves dropped from 115 in 1820 to only 46 in 1840.

At the outbreak of the Civil War Elias removed his slaves from Kiawah, sending them to his Ashepoo plantation, Round-O. In March of 1864 Elias was notified by his factor that he had a $31,754 credit on their books. Six days later he purchased $34,500 of Confederate War Bonds - a tragic mistake that would damage the Vanderhorst fortunes well into the next century.

It is toward the end of the Civil War, in August 1864, that Ann Vanderhorst made a deed out to her son, Arnoldus IV to "give and deliver unto him my slave, a Mulatto Man, named Quash." Piecing together the fragments of history, Quash was apparently Arnoldus' half-brother, being the son of Elias Vanderhorst, Ann's husband. Previously Quash had been at the Round-O plantation, but would from then on be a focal point of activities on Kiawah. There are inconsistencies in the various records, but Quash was apparently born in either May 1840 or 1843.

The Vanderhorst family was broken by the Civil War. Elias and Ann's daughter, Raven, died during the burning of Columbia. They lost virtually all of their possessions and Kiawah was occupied by black freedmen. Elias wrote that, "Nothing was saved in the country, not even my old shoes," and remarked in the same letter, " I hope that Quash remains faithful." Because of Elias' failing health, the day to day operation of Kiawah was taken over by his son, Arnoldus Vanderhorst IV.

In fact, Quash did remain "faithful," although his reasons for doing so are obscure. In 1865 he was writing from Georgetown asking if he should live at Round-O or Kiawah, noting that he could "do well" on either plantation raising cattle. By November 1866 he was on Kiawah, reporting that his potatoes were doing well, but that it was hard to find laborers.

Arnoldus died on December 3, 1881 from a hunting accident. Although newspaper and oral history accounts are at odds, it seems that Quash had previously warned Arnoldus of the "hair trigger" on his shotgun, as well as advised him not to hunt alone. Arnoldus ignored the advice and mortally wounded himself crossing a fallen tree while hunting alone. Others have suggested that, broken by the war and his relentless, yet unsuccessful, efforts to restore Kiawah, Arnoldus committed suicide – an act covered up by the press and inquest which was held in Charleston. Regardless, Kiawah passed to his widow, Adele.

Quash became a prominent figure in the history of Kiawah. He rose from the ranks of a mulatto slave to become both educated (as evidenced by the changing spelling and grammar of his letters) and knowledgeable. He lived his life around the Sea Islands south of Charleston. By 1880, at the age of about 40, census records reveal that he had four children, Eliza (16 years old), William (12 years old), Annie (9 years old), and Laura (7 years old). Although his wife is not listed in the census, Quash speaks of her in his letters.

While Quash was clearly a careful overseer and very dedicated to "Miss

Adele," Kiawah fell into the trap of trying to raise only cotton, while purchasing necessary subsistence crops. Quash's careful oversight and love of Kiawah was also unable to compensate for the ineptitude and disagreeable nature of Adele's son, Arnoldus V, who inherited the island after his mother's death in 1915.

A letter written in 1900 from a relative of Adele Vanderhorst staying on Kiawah commented that Quash was the "Cassique [chief] of Kiawah," and that "he yet bears the loyal affection of the family, whom our branch represents to him, more truly than the young [Arnoldus V] Vanderhorst." The census of that year reveals that Quash had been married to his wife, listed only as J.W. Stevens, for 35 years and that while she had given birth to six children, only two were still alive. The census indicates that both Quash and his wife could read and write. They were still living on Kiawah Island.

The next year Quash left Kiawah, purchasing his own plantation, Seven Oaks, on nearby Johns Island with his son, William F. Stevens. The 839 acre plantation, situated on the Stono River, cost $3,000. Quash's letters express bitter disappointment with the treatment he received from Arnoldus, pointing out that he knew far more about the land and those living on it than did Arnoldus. Apparently Adele interceded and Quash agreed to continue overseeing Kiawah for an additional year while Arnoldus looked for a replacement. Quash's departure from Kiawah marked the end of the island's productivity and a series of white overseers employed by Vanderhorst were never able to restore Kiawah to a place of prominence.

Quash's life after Kiawah is less well known. A plat of the Seven Oaks plantation shows that it contained a number of dwellings, the main settlement, and even a country store. In 1903 Quash and his son sold the timber rights on the plantation to the Dorchester Land and Timber Company for $1,000. Timber deeds such as this were fairly common, providing farmers with ready cash. The renunciation of dower attached to the deed tells us that Quash's wife was Julia W. Stevens and William's wife was Lilla L. Stevens. In November 1909 Quash and William sold Seven Oaks for $3,500. There is no indication in the deed why the plantation was sold, but Quash died on March 20, 1910, only four months later.

His death certificate indicates that he died of heart failure and that he was buried at Centenary Cemetery.

Although little is known of Quash's life, his grandson, Harold Arnoldus Stevens, born on Johns Island, became the first black to hold a seat on the New York State Supreme Court. A newspaper article in 1955 mentioned that his father, presumably William F. Stevens, Quash's only known son, was a blacksmith. Harold Arnoldus Stevens was born on Seven Oaks Farm in 1907 and graduated from Benedict College (in Columbia, S.C.) in 1930. He went on to receive a law degree from Boston College in 1936. At the time of his appointment, he was licensed to practice in both Massachusetts, New York, and South Carolina (suggesting that he maintained his ties with his home state). Harold A. Stevens also served in the New York State Assembly in 1946 and 1948, and in 1950 was named a judge on the General Sessions Court of New York.

Seven Oaks Plantation was the place of bondage of 44 enslaved Africans that lived in 11 cabins on 1100 acres. In 1901 when Quash Stevens and his son William F. Stevens bought Seven Oaks for $3,000 it was only 839 acres. In

1909 Quash Stevens and his son William F. Stevens sold Seven Oaks for $3,500.

The natives that are on the island surrounding Kiawah still seek to have their family members that move north and to other parts of the world to maintain their family ties. Many of these family ties stem from John's Island which is much larger than and neighbors Kiawah. Although some gated areas have started to make their way onto the island, John's Island is still known as a major hub for Gullah/Geechee culture. The families that are now landowners there can look back to their existence in North America coming from the numerous plantations that the island was once divided into. The people on John's Island still tend to live and move about within the boundaries of these same lines of separation that came from these plantation boundaries.

The Rush's Plantation has also been called Ben Roper for one of the owners. This was a later plantation in that it was formed in 1824. This is different than "Rushlands Plantation" on the Stono River off River Road in the vicinity of Rushland Mews and Rushland Landing Road. This was a 924 acre plantation owned by W. Eddings Fripp.

Further down the Stono River is Peaceful Retreat Plantation which was founded in 1719. The British occupied the plantation during the American Revolution and did considerable damage, but they did not burn the house at that time. Later on the original house was burned. This property is often called the "Gibbes Tract" because some of the Gibbes Family were buried on the plantation as late as 1859.

As you continue down the Stono River you will reach the Miller Hill Plantation off River Road in the vicinity of the Miller Hill community and Longwood Plantation off River Road on land now belonging to the Charleston Executive Airport. This 750 acre tract contained 13 buildings for the 47 enslaved Africans of this plantation. It was also called the "Days" Plantation.

"Creekside Plantation" is off River Road, south of the Charleston Executive Airport. These 650 acres housed 135 enslaved Africans in 35 cabins.

Along these banks also lies Fenwich Hall which was named for John Fenwich who built a house there in 1721. This plantation began operation in 1709 and became a harvesting area for Sea Island

Cotton. This once 1,300 acre plantation is now the location of condominiums.

Laurels Plantation or "Simmons Bluff" was 965 acres not far from the 300 acre "Ferry Field Plantation" and "Hanscome Point Plantation." The latter which was a 230 acre home to over 230 enslaved Africans that lived in 59 cabins is now a gated area.

"Exchange Plantation" also on the Stono River at the northwest corner of River Road and Plowground Road contained 560 acres in 1865. During its years as a functioning plantation at least 170 enslaved people dwelled there in 48 cabins.

"Adasville Plantation" on the Stono River and off Chisolm Road in the vicinity of Blue Cross Lane was also called "Becketts." In 1910 the *Blue Cross Union Society* had 1/2 acre of the property, but was able to obtain a much larger tract from later on. It appears that they obtained approximately 1/2 of the original 1,000 acre plantation.

"Oakvale Plantation" off River Road (SC 45) on Burden Creek Road and Kemway Road has also been called Burden's. It is now a Stono Point where gated exclusionism has replaced sea island cotton fields.

"Belvidere Plantation" located off Chisolm Road in the vicinity of Gift Boulevard and Belvedere Road. It has also been called Gift, Laurel Point, Mount Pleasant, and Waterside since it began in 1708. It is along the Stono River with "Blacklock Plantation" which was a 551 acre sea island cotton plantation.

Stono River was also home to "Indigo Point Plantation" often called "Maryville," "Silk Hope," or "Sylcope." These 720 acres were along the banks just as the "Bluff Plantation" which also harvested indigo and later cotton was. Bluff was where Colonel Lucas Pinckney enslaved at least 20 Africans.

"Auld Reeckie Plantation" off River Road in the vicinity of Edenborough, Auldreeke, and Sunnyside Farm Roads has been called "Old Home Place" and "Old Homestead." The seventy enslaved Africans forced to dwell in the twenty cabins may not have called it as such a genteel name.

"White Hall Plantation" is on Abbapoola Creek. Thomas Porcher had a house built on these 425 acres in 1866. He also made sure that a tavern was there for travelers. "Indian Graves Plantation" is a 250 acre plot further down the creek on the East bank. The Mathewes operated this area of enslavement as well as "Contentment Hall Plantation" off Legareville Road. The latter was a 329 acre enslavement area that housed 45 Africans in 15 cabins. "Brick House Plantation" which has also been referred to as "Stanyarne's" or "Stanyarne Hall" was a 500 acre plantation also along these banks.

"Townsends Plantation" on Bohicket Creek (a branch of the North Edisto River) was a 226 acre plantation settled in 1865 by the Jenkins. Off Betsy Kerrison Parkway is the 644 acre "Hopkinson Plantation" or "Live Oak Point." "Hickory Hill Plantation" on this creek was an 1,800 acre cotton plantation in 1865. Down the water was the 982 acre Fair Oaks Plantation and the 1,000 acre "Angels-Hoopstick Plantation." The latter enslaved at least 40 Africans who dwelled in 18 cabins. "Orange Hill Plantation" off Edenvale Road which was owned by the Fripps had a greater population of enslaved people with less housing. There are only 4 cabins documented, but a population of 60 enslaved people.

"Hut Plantation" is on Hut Creek (a branch of the Stono River) off River Road near Hut Road. This 639 acres has been owned by Kinsey Burden, the Harlestons, and the Robertsons.

All of these names can still be seen throughout Charleston and in various historical context.

"Hope Plantation" on Haulover Creek (a branch of the Kiawah River) off Betsy Kerrison Parkway on Hope Plantation Drive is a gated area which was also once called "DuPre." These 559 acres can now potential assist in the re-enslaving of the Gullah/Geechees of the island as taxes rise because of these types of residential designs.

Edenvale Road takes its name from the 434 acre plantation that was there also. Solomon Legare, Jr. owned this estate. Taking a drive from there along Church Creek near Chisolm Road and Mary Ann Point Road will lead to the 1,000 acre "Deer Park Plantation" that the Wilsons owned.

"Back Pen Plantation" on Church Creek (a branch of the Wadmalaw River) was also called "Pond." It began in 1790 as 1,040 acres bound by what is now Main Road and Chisolm.

"Briars Plantation" on the Kiawah River at Legareville was 764. 46 enslaved Africans once occupied the 29 Slave cabins there.

"Myrtles Plantation," "Murray-Gibbes Plantation," "Curtis Hall," "Capes Plantation," "Cane Slash," and "California Plantations" are also on Johns Island. The latter is off Main Road in the vicinity of California Lane and Doctor Whaley Road. It was once the 1,017 acre "Turkey Hill Plantation" where 85 cabins were the homes of 105 enslaved Africans. "Curtis Hall Plantation" off Maybank Highway near Main Road. "Oaks Plantation" was 1,200 acres which was worked by approximate 100 enslaved Africans. Amongst themselves, they split 29 cabins.

"Mullet Hall Plantation" at Legareville was 727 in 1865. Prior to this time it was the home of 110 enslaved Africans that dwelled in the 30 cabins there.

Continue across the river to Wadamalaw Island and find a place lined with plantations including "Rocks" (which was a cotton plantation), "Cottage Plantation," "Bears Bluff Plantation," and "New Cut Plantation." The latter derived its name from a cut, dug by hand through the marsh and mud to allow the passage of boats from Church Creek to the Stono River. It was first formed in 1842.

"Yellow House Plantation" was a 603 acre plantation that was operated by 43 enslaved people that dwelled in 8 cabins. "Bugby Plantation" on Bohicket Creek down from "Anchorage Plantation" off Maybank Highway on Bugby Road was also called "Quiet Corner." The 102 acres that began to be built up in 1940 was operated by 26 enslaved Africans that dwelled in the nine cabins there. Down from it was "Acorn Hill Plantation" which began in 1860 just before the plantation era would end. The 25 people enslaved there at that time worked the 600 acre rice plantation by hand. "Rosebank Plantation" was formed there in 1821 as a 1200 acre cotton plantation.

The "Charleston Tea Plantation" is a functioning tea plantation that was sold to the *Lipton Company*. The primary crop there is what goes into "American Classic Tea."

"Allendale Plantation" on Leadenwah Creek came into existence in 1855. However, long before it, "Oak Grove Plantation" was along these banks functioning as a 700 acre rice plantation. It was established in 1767.

Little Edisto Island is not always heard of from those that do not live right near it, but it also played its part in the plantation system. "Windsor Plantation" on Russell Creek, East of SC 174 was also called "Ashwood." It started in 1847 as a 141 acre cotton plantation tended by 68 enslaved Africans.

Also on the Edisto River is "Clifton Plantation," "Cypress Trees Plantation," and Pine Island which was a plantation unto itself. "Oak Hurst Plantation" was located on both sides of the South Edisto River. The main portion was on the east shore north of Willtown Bluff. The island was on the west shore bounded by Hope Creek. This area that was also called "Hutton" was a rice plantation as early as 1714.

"Summit Plantation" on Swinton Creek in Adams Run is off Toogoodoo Road. Amarinthia Jenkins named the plantation "Summit" because it expressed the summit of her happiness. Those that began being enslaved there in 1594 and worked harvesting rice my not have shared her joy. It was originally granted to Landgrave Thomas Smith in 1694 and re-granted to Joseph Blake six years later. In 1730 John Bull built a house there, but the original house fell into disrepair and was known as "Rat Hall." So in 1819 a new home was built by William Wilkinson. In the years to come, this how would be surrounded by cotton fields.

"Grove Plantation" in Adams Run east of Willtown Bluff off Jehossee Island Road was a 1112 acre rice plantation on which at least 136 Africans were enslaved. This is now a part of the *ACE Basin National Wildlife Refuge*.

"Jehossee Plantation" was the entire Jehossee Island on the South Edisto River on which Governor William Aiken enslaved Africans to cultivate rice. He later expanded into cattle, sweet potatoes, and corn. The original property was bounded on the west by the South Edisto River, on the north and east by the Dawho River, and on the south by the Intracoastal Waterway. It has been also written about as "Jehosea." This is now a part of the *ACE Basin National Wildlife Refuge*.

"Lem's Bluff Plantation" in Willtown was a land granted to Landgrave Joseph Morton. This later became a cotton plantation. "Willtown Bluff Plantation" off SC 164 on Willtown Road also began in 1714. Initially a place called "New London" which came to be called "Willtown Bluff" was established in 1685 on the Edisto River. When a land grant was issued to Landgrave Robert Daniel these 1016 acres became a rice plantation. However, before this occurred, "London on the Edisto" was a town or frontier settlement.

Laurel Hill Plantation in Ravenel is also called "Laurel Hill Settlement." It is a 390 acre rice plantation which was a part of a 1711 land grant to a man named Elliot is now a part of the Charleston County Park and Recreation Commission's Caw Caw Interpretive Center along with Stanyarne Hill Plantation which was between the Home Tract and Coates Settlement. This portion was once 1,182 acres.

Barings Plantation on South Edisto River was bounded to the south by Penny Creek, to the north by US 17, and to the west by the South Edisto River. It was named after Charles Baring II who owned it in the 1830s. It was a rice plantation at its height.

Only parts of Edisto Island are in Charleston County today. It has had it own number of divisions since it became a location of plantations as well. "Bayview" and "Governor's Bluff" are amongst them. "Prospect Hill Plantation" located one mile west of SC 174 off Parkers Ferry Road is now primarily owned by *McLeod Lumber Company*. In 1790 it was a rice plantation.

"Point of Pines Plantation" off SC 174 on Point of Pines Road is also called "Mitchell Place." It sprang from a 1,000 acre land grant in 1674. Sea Island Cotton became its primary crop. The plantation has the remains of three slave cabins on Edisto Island which can still be seen near the river.

Old House Plantation about a mile east of SC 174 got its name when Brick House burned and it became the oldest dwelling still intact on the island. It has also been called "Four Chimneys." The cotton plantation began in 1735 and William Jenkins built a house there in 1750. Extensive renovations were made by the Seabrooks in the early 19th century, mostly to the interior.

"Oak Island Plantation" on Westbank Creek (a branch of the North Edisto River) came into existence in 1828 and William Seabrook, Jr. built the house there in 1830. From 1862 to 1865 Union troops occupied the plantation house. However, prior to their arrival these 347 acres were a harvesting site of sea island cotton. "Slann Island Plantation" was another island on the

Dawho River. This was a 375 acre sea island cotton and rice plantation that was owned by Captain William Seabrook.

Peters Point Plantation on St Pierre Creek was also called "Point Saint Pierre." The sea island cotton plantation started in 1821 and was also a place of occupation for Union troops. The 225 enslaved Africans no doubt preferred their presence to those that had been there before.

"Middleton's Plantation" on Store Creek is about three miles west of SC 174. The sea island cotton plantation was also called "The Launch" and "Chisolm's." The latter name came long after the 1795 establishment of the plantation due to the ownership changing hands to Dr. Robert Trail Chisolm who built a house there in the 1800s.

"Laurel Hill Plantation" on Toogoodoo Creek (a branch of the North Edisto River) was a 195 acre plantation.

"Tom Seabrook Plantation" was named for Thomas Bannister Seabrook. This became a sea island cotton plantation.

"Frogmore Plantation" which started in 1820 as yet another home to sea island cotton. It also was the home of 124 enslaved Africans.

"Baynard's Old Place Plantation" on Russell Creek (a branch of the North Edisto River) is named for the Baynard family. It has also been referred to as "Mr. Charles Seabrook's Place," "Seabrook Place," and Pine Ridge. It began in 1772 and was enlarged as the sea island cotton plantation expanded.

"Bleak Hall Plantation" on Ocella Creek (a branch of the North Edisto River) was home to 273 enslaved Africans that toiled in sea island cotton. Before it came into existence, "Brookland Plantation" on St Pierre Creek off Laurel Hill Road, southwest of SC 174 was already established. This area also called "Hill Tract," "Brooklands," or "Brooklines" came into existence in 1789 as an indigo plantation. However, the latter names for it came from it becoming a boys' home after the property was auctioned off for taxes. In 1968 the *Brookland Home for Boys* was moved near Orangeburg.

"Cassina Point Plantation" off Clark Road on Cassina Point Road was a sea island cotton plantation called "Hopkinson House." The house there was built for William Seabrook's daughter, Carolina Lafayette and her husband,

John Hopkinson.

"Crawford Plantation" on Fishing Creek at 8202 Oyster Factory Road off SC 174 was named after James Crawford that may have started it as a sea island plantation in 1784.

The 1,240 acre "Sea Cloud Plantation"'s name came through the marriage of a member of the Seabrook family to a member of the McLeod family. Rice was the claim to fame of this plantation. However, "Seabrook Plantation" on Steamboat Creek (a branch of the North Edisto River), located about a mile west of SC 174 began in 1810 as a sea island cotton plantation.

"Seaside Plantation" began in 1790. The Fripp Family built a home there. They were then surrounded by the 120 enslaved Africans of the plantation.

"Lexington Plantation" on Wando Neck is also called "Four Men's Ramble." Although this is now a part of *Dunes West Golf Club,* before 1670, according to the history of the golf club: "The Europeans referred to the Indians of the Wando Neck as the 'Sewee' and the 'Wando.' The seagoing Sewee may have built a fortified village along the Wando not far from this site." In 1696 a 1,000 acre grant was made to

Landgrave Edmund Bellinger, who apparently did not develop the property. In 1704 he sold it to Major Alexander Parris who in 1712 sold it to Captain John Vanderhorst, Joseph Vanderhorst, and Thomas Lynch. Lynch's grandson, Thomas Lynch Jr., signed the *Declaration of Independ- ence*.

In 1738 Captain John Vanderhorst died and bequeathed his share of the plantation to Arnoldus Vanderhorst. In 1754 Arnoldus Vanderhorst owned all the land between Toomer and Wagner Creeks. In 1765 Arnoldus Vanderhorst left the property to Colonel Arnoldus Vanderhorst II, who owned plantation until his death in 1802. Vanderhorst also owned much of Kiawah Island.

In 1827 the plantation was sold to A.S. Willington, first editor of the *Charleston News and Courier* and it became known as "Lexington." In 1830 it was purchased by Effingham Wagner, who died in 1837.

In 1861, Wagner's widow Emma sold plantation to Captain Paul Waring Jr. In 1863 Captain Waring died in battle; Emma Wagner bought Lexington back. From 1857 to 1902 it was owned by James McElroy.

By the end of the Civil War, the main

house was in ruins; it may have been burned by Union soldiers. However, in 1930, one of America's wealthiest women, Henrietta Hartford, widow of Edward V. Hartford bought it. Mrs. Hartford built a 32-room home where the original house had been, and she planted an avenue of oaks. At this time, she also added a saltwater swimming pool, tennis courts, a nine-hole golf course, stables, a guest house, and servants quarters. Her gardens were designed by the Olmsted firm. (Frederick Law Olmsted was a landscape architect who also designed the Biltmore Estate in Asheville, Central Gardens in New York City, and Cherokee Plantation in Colleton County.) Mrs. Hartford married Prince Guido Pignatelli of Italy in 1937 and thus became Princess Pignatelli.

In 1942 the house mysteriously burned. In 1947 the O.L. Williams Veneer Company bought it and it later became part of Georgia Pacific / Destination Wild Dunes. In 1991 the Scratch Gold Company acquired the property and created *Dunes West Golf Club*. The clubhouse was built on site of original big house and outbuildings of this previously 1,000 acre cotton and rice plantation. This site also produced bricks. These were no doubt constructed by the 80 or so enslaved Africans that dwelled in the twenty cabins there.

The Charleston Neck or just "The Neck" is the narrow or neck of the Charleston peninsula just north of the city, bound on one side by the Ashley River and on the other side by the Cooper River. It was the location of the "Sans Souci Plantation" and was even called "Sans Souci-on-the-Ashley." It began in 1799. Belvidere Plantation is also there near the Magnolia Cemetery. It began in 1795. A golf course is now on the property. Belmont on the Cooper River in the Neck was owned by Colonel Pinckney and the house he had built was destroyed between 1780 and 1785.

The Charleston Army Depot on was once the "Cooper River Palmetto Plantation." "Villa Plantation" on the eastern branch of the Cooper River has been credited with being where John Guerard invented the first rice pounding mill in America in 1691. "Coté Bas Plantation" also along these banks came about in 1712.

"Childermas Croft Plantation" also on The Neck is now an industrial area. Nothing remains of the 218 acre 1735 plantation other than a small burial site. Childermas Croft served in many appointed positions such as Notary Public, Clerk of Crown, Chief Justice, etc. and owned a number of enslaved people.

"Live Oak Plantation" on Rantowles Creek twelve miles from Charleston, once a part of the Colonel William Washington tract. This was a rice plantation.

Red Top area off US Highway 17 contained "Bulow Plantation" on Rantowles Creek. As of January 2005 50 acres of land and 300 acres of marsh on Bulow Plantation were placed under a Ducks Unlimited Conservation Easement. This is only a portion of the original 600 acre plantation.

Hollywood, SC consist of "Dixie Plantation" on the Stono River off of SC 162 on Plantation Road. Since this was originally Colleton County information about it is limited due to the records of Colleton County being loss by fire during the Civil War. The December 12, 2002, *Charleston Mercury*, contained "The Dixie Dilemma," which stated: "The Issues, First, John Henry Dick left no endowment for Dixie Plantation. Second, Mr. Dick left Dixie to College of Charleston Foundation, not the college itself. And third, for all the people who claim to know what Mr. Dick intended, he seemed to have left a clear indication of his plan for Dixie's future when he placed an easement on the property in 1993 with the Lowcountry Open Land Trust."

The new plans for the formerly 800 acre plantation include creating a walking trail through the property with field lab sites set up along the trail and buildings in the upper corner of the property where most of the construction would be confined. Construction at the plantation is limited because of the easement that requires low intensity educational uses.

There is a two story house, a brick garage with servant quarters and a clapboard guest house with four rooms. In addition, there are the usual outbuildings and tenant house. The property contains the family cemetery. The avenue of oaks is attributed to the Seabrook family who built a large mansion at the end of the drive.

The issue over this plantation and the usage of it will no doubt take years to contend with. The people of James Island are used to having to deal with these same issues of usage and zoning as they continue to battle with the

City of Charleston in court in order to have their own township with their own town council. This council existed for a short period of time and then was overturned as the City of Charleston sought to annex portions of the island into its boundaries which would place it under control of the Charleston City Council.

The irony of this issue prevailing in the 200s is that the Council of the Province was given an order to create a town on James Island in 1671. It contained 12,000 acres and was to be named "James Town" in honor of James, Duke of York. This town was never mapped on "Boone Island" or "James Island" as it is now known. However, the seventeen plantation that were there are.

"Dill's Bluff" owned by Dill and then Rhett was amongst the many plantations on James Island. "Turquetts Plantation" became combined with "Stono Plantation." The primary crop there was indigo which 45 enslaved Africans harvest. Twihets Plantation was 224 acres. "Stiles Point Plantation" on the Ashley River at 940 Paul Revere Drive came about in 1741 as a sea island cotton plantation. Later cabbage and green beans were farmed there. "McLeod

Plantation" is the last of these historic plantations that remains in tact.

McLeod Plantation began in 1741 as 617 acres of land was sold to William Wilkins. The land was used as a cattle station at that time. Open grazing cattle farming was one of the skills that the Africans brought with them in the hulls of the ships. Therefore, it was easy for them to operate this space. The beef and pork raised on this island was sold to the islands of the Caribbean for the most part. Later the island took on indigo as a primary crop.

William Wilkins who was born in Nevis in the Caribbean settled on James Island and purchased this parcel of land. Wilkins became the highway commissioner, tax inquirer and inquisitor, road commissioner, justice of the peace, a member of the grand jury for James Island, and a member of the Seventeenth Assembly from 1720 to 1721. Wilkins sold and repurchased this land several times. He sold it to Samuel Perronneau who engaged in selling dry goods and fabrics including "Negro cloth" in Charleston. A store was also once mapped on the property of McLeod. Perronneau also operated in the importation of Africans.

Perronneau had land on Edisto Island as well. His estate focused on cattle, swine, and sheep. In his will he wanted his executor to "purchase for the use and behoof of the same such a number of Slaves as to Enable them to settle plant & occupy my Plantation & Lands at James Island in this Province with twelve Working Slaves." Perronneau's daughter would not have any trouble fulfilling her father's wishes given that she married, Edward Lightwood Jr. who along with Thomas Eveleigh engaged in the trade of human cargo.

In 1767 Edward Lightwood acquired the property and had a home there by 1780. The Lightwoods and Parker Families sold the property to William Wallace McLeod in 1851. McLeod expanded business here and enslaved seventy-four to one hundred African people who successfully grew sea island cotton.

The twenty-three enslavement cabins that were built over the years were where many families of James Island still lived well into the 1950s. There are few of these cabins still standing as parts of the estate have been sold over the years.

The original plantation house was

replaced by a home for the McLeod's in 1854. This house was used as a hospital, regimental headquarters, and commissary by the Confederates and Union during the Civil War. The 55th Massachusetts Volunteers was stationed at this site. This later became an office of the

Freedmen's Bureau during Reconstruction. This bureau assisted the Gullah/Geechees that now owned from five to twenty acres each with land issues, food, clothing, etc.

Battery Means was constructed on McLeod Plantation after McLeod had taken his family northward to safety. This was to be a defense for the Charleston Harbor. This portion of the plantation is now a part of the "Country Club of Charleston." The clubhouse terrace runs along the boundary of the battery.

McLeod Plantation was the center of the *"James Island Agricultural Society"* which was formed in 1871. This society focused on coordinating labor relations on the island and ways to make sea island cotton competitive in the face of the increased cultivation of upland cotton. They eventually started providing agricultural scholarships. As the boll weevil destroyed the cotton crops, vegetables such as asparagus, cabbage, and Irish potatoes that could be truck farmed became the focus. However, the McLeods could not keep this going with less and less people willing to work their fields. So, the period of 1918 to 1940 marked the end of the McLeod's farming industry. William Ellis McLeod then leased out a part of the land to others for them to grow soybeans and other crops on.

The Gullah/Geechees of James Island had a paramilitary group called *The Hunter Volunteers.*" They were centered at McLeod Plantation as well. Today a different type of group has been formed to rally to protect McLeod Plantation. This multicultural group is called *"Friends of McLeod."* This non-profit organization (www.mcleodplantation.org) has been advocating for McLeod to remain as a sacred historic space for the Gullah/Geechee Nation. The *City of Charleston* sold the property to the "School of the Building Arts" that seeks to build new buildings amidst those that currently exist. However, this will change the historic integrity of the space which should be kept open for the Gullah/Geechee spirits that are buried there to rest peacefully and to speak to living souls that journey there to pay homage.

"Dixon's Island Plantation" is an island adjacent to James Island. This was the site of a skirmish in May of 1862 during the Civil War as were many of the lands around James Island including McLeod Plantation. Thus, on January 3, 1863, Owner William H. Taylor appeared before Magistrate M.E. Rivers to claim property losses resulting from Union occupation in June of 1862:

The State of South Carolina
Charleston District

Personally appeared before me William H. Taylor & made oath that all of the buildings on his Plantation known as Dixon's Island a small Island adjacent to James Island were destroyed by the Enemy in June last during the time that they occupied a portion of James Island & that said buildings consisting of a Dwelling House, Kitchen, Corn House & Dairy were worth to this Deponent at least the sum of One Thousand Dollars. Deponent further swears that upon his said Plantation or Island were three head of cattle which he was prohibited from removing by the order of the General in command of James Island assigning as a reason that they would be wanted for the use of the troops under his command, that he has made frequent application to the military authorities for payment for said cattle, but up to the present time has received no satisfaction whatever so that they also have been a total loss to this deponent – that at the rate such cattle were then selling they would have been worth at least One Hundred and Sixty five Dollars. Deponent therefore estimates his entire loss at Eleven Hundred and Sixty five Dollars & prays relief –

    Sworn to before me
    this 3rd Jany 1863
Wm.H. Taylor

    M.E. Rivers
    Magistrate

This would end as the plantation "goods" and "property" would also occupy these buildings that they had built and the lands that had surrounded them. The day of Jubilee had final come and freedom was all that those who had been enslaved could see now growing from these grounds!

Lass Gwine Be Fuss: Wi Fight fa Freedum

> "Rise like lions after slumber,
> In unconquerable number!
> Shake to earth your chains, like dew
> Which in sleep had fallen on you!
> Ye are many!   They are few!"
>
> •by Shelley

As the system and cycle of enslavement grew in the colonies, the mechanisms to keep that system in tact and running consistently to benefit the few were institutionalized through numerous codes and laws. The more that the enslaved multiplied, the more concerns developed that they would also rise against this system. If they started to realize at any point that they were in sufficient numbers and in close enough proximity to each other to fully take over this system and re-establish their own freedom, the Anglos in their midst feared this not only being the downfall of the entire structure that their lives and livelihood had been based on, but they also feared massive slaughters in retaliation would take place.

Initially Africans of different ethnic groups were brought to enslavement pens and on board ships and were blended with Africans from other countries and regions. This was a mechanism not only utilize to secure variations in the skills of the enslaved, but also as a means by which to keep them from communicating with one another. This attempt backfired due to the creation of the Gullah language by the Africans. The Africans blended their languages and created this language which some linguist argue had its conception in the holding pens that were along the coast of the Western seaboard of Alkebulan which we call Africa today. It seemed to be an outgrowth of a trade language that was already available to the Africans as they moved about over land and sea to conduct trade amongst them- selves and with other ethnic groups in other parts of the world. The gestation took place in the sweltering confines of the enslavement pens and yards with waters of the Middle Passage being the amniotic fluid that contained it. However, the soils of the Sea Islands would be the womb that would erupt to bring it forth. This same womb would erupt and bring back the collective consciousness of freedom.

From the time that Africans encountered the invaders on their own shores, they fought. As they were brought across the Atlantic Ocean through the Middle Passage, they fought. This fighting spirit was what the enslavers felt had to be quelled if their captives were to remain within their bondage and become tools of the economic flow that needed to be established.

Given that the Europeans had already been enslaving Africans in the islands that would come to be called both the "West Indies" and the "Caribbean," they had witnessed a number of uprisings. These uprising produced not only work stoppages, the burning of cash crops and buildings, but also the deaths of many of those that were the plantation owners. Thus, for the enslaved Africans that did not succumb to the physical shock of being kidnapped and transported nor to the diseases within the hulls of the ships nor to the suicidal melancholia brought on by plantation conditions, there had to be a means by which to keep them "in their place."

One of the first processing procedures of enslavement was to "season" the enslaved. After being unloaded at the "pestilence houses" which are called "pest houses" of Sullivan's Island the enslaved would often go through a process of preparation not only for sale, but also for plantation life. Those that appeared to still have a warrior spirit were often beaten and even starved so that they would either have their wills broken or would be so weak, that they would appear to have been broken down and "whipped into shape."

After leaving the denigrating stands of the "slave auction blocks" that once were disbursed all over the streets of the Charleston peninsula (It was in the latter years of the system that indoor markets such as the one that is called "The Slave Mart Museum" on Chalmers Street today were built and operated.), the Africans then were taken to their places of bondage. There the Africans used their skills and knowledge to clear land, split boards and build buildings with these and the bricks that they also made by hand. They were then able to devise how to construct fields that would produce massive quantities of what were later to be deemed the "cash crops"-indigo, long staple Sea Island cotton, and Carolina Gold rice.

As with any system of production and exchange of goods, their have to be engineers. These were the enslaved Africans. Many of them had been purposely enslaved because of their skill levels and what they had been producing in their own homeland for their own people or in other African villages where they may have been captives of war themselves.

The skills ranged from blacksmithing, to architecture, to agriculture, herbology, astronomy (or astrology depending on how one looks at the studies of the cosmological bodies) to boat building and more. In order to insure that production is efficient, there are those that must be placed in charge. More often than not, those that were left in charge of the areas that came to be called "plantations" were not the so-called owners of the land and the chattel (as the enslaved were considered to be). In fact, those in charge were the overseers and the drivers.

"Slave codes" dictated that overseers be white. However, many plantations were run by drivers. More oft than not, these drivers were actually the children of a sexual encounter between the enslaved woman and a plantation owner. As a result, a profile developed for those that fell into this category and on average they were 25 to 35 years old and considered of "mixed blood" or "mulatto." If for any reason there was a low amount of mulattos that could be entrusted with this position, then a newly arriving African could be chosen or a first generation born enslaved individual may get this position. Nat Weaver was a freeman that worked as a driver at Elias Ball's "Limerick Plantation."

On average there was one driver to 50 other enslaved people. Many times they were the only ones allowed to wear blue and everyone else wore white. Also, they were usually the only ones watches and access to liquor. This would be an element of discussions as later "slave codes" were developed, but it could not have been of major concern to plantation owners that used drivers given the fact that they were already breaking the code or law by not utilizing overseers.

Even with drivers and overseers in place, the Africans whose hearts remained in tact always beat out a rhythm of return to freedom and to their Motherland. They used both overt and covert means of undermining the system that they were the primary instruments in. As a result, the writers of the day would try to quietly deal with the problems that they faced with escapees and what they considered indignation amongst some of the enslaved.

1721 an act for "maintaining a Watch and keeping Good Orders in Charles Town" was passed because whites did not like blacks coming into the town on Sundays and drinking, fighting, and gathering. If the blacks were in public after 9 pm, they could be confined in a cage until the next morning and if they did not stop when called, they could be shot.

In 1737 another act passed again requiring a pass and a lantern if they were out past 8 pm in the winter and past 9 pm in the summer. The ticket was to state their precise business in the city. If caught without this, they would be placed in a watch house until the morning and then publicly whipped the next day. The owner would be fined five shillings due to this violation.

"No Negroes were allowed on the streets of the city between drum- beat at night (retreat) and drum-beat in the morning (reveille). A chief duty of the police was to arrest any one then found unless indeed he was provided with a pass (called a ticket), signed by his owner or a member of his owner's family. The morning drum-beat took place at daybreak; and in the evening at quarter past ten o'clock in summer, and quarter past nine in the winter. The drum was beaten at the main door of the Guardhouse on Broad Street by a negro man named Peter Brown, and he was assisted by a less important darkey who played the fife. This military signal was preceded on the stroke of the hour by the 'bell-ring,' which lasted for fifteen minutes. 'First bell-ring' was always two hours ahead of 'last bell-ring,' say at seven in winter and nine o'clock in summer, and corresponded, I suppose to 'tattoo.' During the day the negroes were restrained from going where they pleased by a master's orders or by the needs of their daily routine of service. There were no latch-keys or night-locks in those days, and one of the men servants had to sit up to 'answer the bell' until every member of the family was at home, and it was too late for visitors, when they locked up the house and retired to their own quarters. In our house the footmen performed this night-duty by turns. It was considered rather un- civilized for the servants to sleep under the same roof with 'the family,' and in every yard there were outhouses built especially to accommodate them. In the lowest story of one of these was the cook-kitchen, and wash-kitchen, the former being nearest the house. In one yard the servants were sometimes allowed to have dancing in the evening, to which their friends came, but they always broke up at drum-beat, so as to get home before that ceased.

Many negroes, especially the mechanics, were allowed to 'work out' or to 'hire their own time.' For these the city authorities issued a license, as was and still is done in many occupations.

A most ridiculous trade is to-day carried on in the curiosity shops, which sell the very ordinary bits of brass as 'slave-badges' at high prices, the number being supposed, I believe, to represent the slave's number on his master's plantation or in his household, just as a convict is known by his number in a penitentiary! Doubtless many of these commonplace licenses have been dispersed over the North as curiosities of slavery!

The jurisdiction of the master over the slave for small offenses did not cease in the city, but the punishment was inflicted in an orderly way by a police official at a public institution called the work-house.

The white man, adjudged by a court to a whipping, received his punishment in the market place in the presence of the Sheriff or his deputy as previously mentioned.

A good deal of money in a small way circulated among the negroes, and the keepers of the smaller grocery shops made a good profit out of his trade. These were chiefly Germans, who in many cases were bold breakers of the law against selling liquor to the blacks. I remember as a little boy once seeing old Frank lead out of the dining room an intoxicated Tony, who remembered how-ever that 'honor rooted in dishonor stood,' and resolutely refused to give the name of the vendor. These shops were always at corners, and were called "Dutchman cornershops.' This aspersion on the Hollander was very unjust, for of them there were few and they were merchants of standing and repute.

The negro children in town were, as on plantations, carefully trained. The girls were often sent to sewing schools or to pastry-cooks. Such as school was kept near us was named Nannie Cross, and her specialists were rather cakes of various sorts. Bob and I as little chaps would club our money and get there one saucer of ice-cream with two spoons, which we ate in a little arbour with old Nannie (an f.p.c.) beaming affection over us.

The fourth of July was very grand féte

for the negroes. The military parade always took place on account of the heat very early in the morning, and was dismissed with the firing of three volleys on the East Battery. On Meeting Street from Chalmers Street to the South Battery and along the South Battery the sidewalks were crowded with booths kept by old negro maumas, and many more were under the trees on the Battery." (p. 94-95 Smith, Alice Huger, "A Carolina Rice Plantation of the Fifties" 1936 William Morrow and Company New York, NY)

Celebrations were and still remain a way in which people of African descent break from the psychological strains and chains placed upon them due to oppression. On a regular basis, the enslaved Africans sought ways to break the chains in which they were physically bound as well. One of many examples occurred in

August of 1730 when a two-fold uprising was planned. One part was designed for an enslaved African in each family was to murder his or her enslaver and all other white men and women in the middle of the night. The other part was that there would be an assembly that they would call a "Dancing-Bout." Proper preparations would be made so that they would the rush in and take over the city. They would use all arms and ammunition that they could obtain to kill all Anglo people. The leaders were taken the night of the gathering and many of them were executed which did not allow the plan to go forth.

In January 1761, The South Carolina Gazette reported that "The negroes it seems have again begun the hellish practice of poisoning." This process was in practice throughout the Sea Islands and can often be heard of even in Gullah/Geechee general conversations at the present time. In order to address such incidents, people were not only beaten, but also issued the death penalty. They hung a male and female on "Wadmalah(w)" Island for this.

In McClellanville a Gullah/Geechee girl named, Jemima murdered her female enslaver who was a widow named, Perderiau. Jemima tied up the children and also took what she could from the house. However, the children got loose and went to Colonel Warren who got a posse of men together and went after her. When they found her gathered amongst her people, they took her and then burned her at the stake.

Brutality against the Gullah/Geechees

continued and is documented in each area in many cases. The names are not usually recorded because killing someone of African descent was not considered a true crime at the time. It was written in McClellanville of how Mr. Benjamin Fort shot a Negro on his piazza one night after the war and Mr. Charles McCay shot one near Palmer's Bridge. It was always assumed that the Anglo person had the right to do these things. By the same token, the Africans no doubt continued to know that they had the right to do what they could to be free.

No doubt due to the ever increasing fears of the Anglos, a number of laws and codes started to develop during the 1700s. In addition to laws that governed the activities of the enslaved, the enslaved were utilized as "curio" items and sources of entertainment. "In the streets of Charleston a curfew for Negroes was enforced. Any Negro found walking about after dusk without a written permit from his master or mistress was arrested. Owners often made extra money by hiring out their domestic slaves, who were then given a copper identity disc bearing name, date and occupation to wear. Albino Negroes and mulattoes were exhibited for money as freaks or curiosities- a Gazette advertisement for May 1743 announces one such exhibition at the house of Mr. Joel Poinsett in Charleston. Mr. Poinsett was showing for a week in June, and for five shillings a head entrance fee, a 'WHITE Negro girl, of Negro parents, she is as white as any European, has a lovely blush in her countenance, grey eyes continually trembling, and hair fisled [sic] as the wool of a white lamb'." ("Sins of the Fathers: A Study of the Atlantic Slave Traders 1441-1807 by James Pope-Hennessy 1967 Pope-Hennessy-1998 Barnes and Noble Inc. NY p. 228)

This fascination with Africans as sources of entertainment and curiosity continued into 1858 when the South Carolina State Fair had "new Africans" on display. Many that come to the Gullah/Geechee Nation at the present time often come to also gaze at the "peculiar people" that they have heard legends about through thesis papers that have become published works or documentaries and feature length films that only depict the Gullah/Geechees as entertainers or people of odd fetishes.

Just as many Gullah/Geechees continued to express their efforts toward freedom through a complex system of efforts that still incorporate mechanisms that their ancestors utilized on their plantations, the enslaved Africans must have taken pride in what they knew would be a strong fruit seed if they planted freedom in the collective consciousness of their group. Those that first harvested these seeds took stands on their own and continued to "steal away" to other areas along with indigenous Americans (Many of whom are called "Seminole" today are of this group.) and others set out on their own to find freedom in other lands or to attempt to make it back to their homelands.

"In South Carolina there was never a time when organized attempts at black uprisings did not seem a part of the land-scape, a subject of white fears. In 1720 authorities in Charleston discovered a plot 'of the negroes with a design to destroy all the white people in the country and then to take the town.' A few years later a minister in Goose Creek Parish complained of 'secret poisonings and bloody insurrection by certain Christian slaves'." ("There is a River: The Struggle for Freedom in America" by Vincent Harding 1981 Harcourt Brace & Company p. 33)

From 1735 to 1739 11,000 Africans came through Sullivan's Island. More than 8,000 were from the Angola region. While the British sought to bring in more and more "black cargo" or "black gold" to further enrich themselves, the indigenous Americans of the area sought ways to try to work between them and the Spanish of La Florida in such a way to turn things back toward their advantage. In 1727 it has been documented that a raiding party was sent to Carolina by the Spanish Governor. This party consisted of Yamassees. They would receive "thirty pieces of eight for every English scalp and one hundred for every live Negro they should bring."

These raiding parties sometimes ended up in battles with the Anglos that wanted to retain "their property." However, in other cases, they were able to get away with the "Negroes" in tow. Some came by land and some by schooner. No matter which means would take them to freedom, the Africans were willing to go. As a result, the Anglos started to set up mechanisms for bounties to be paid for all the Negroes that were recaptured and returned to Carolina. Yet, some never returned and became those that settled "Pueblo de Gracia de Real de Santa Teresa de Mose" or

"Moosa" as this area near today's St. Augustine, Florida was called. A historical marker now stands at the location of "Fort Mosé" to honor those that held this ground.

The Africans who led the Stono Rebellion were heading to this Florida township in which "Negroes" were to be free. Jemmy or Cato who was the leader was a recent arrival into the area and bonded quickly with the people. On September 9, 1739, Cato lead what would go down in history at the "Stono Rebellion."

Charlestown had been trying to recover from a yellow fever epidemic that had run through the area for months. There had also been two other major uprising attempts. Yet, in the early morning of September 9, 1739, the enslaved Africans rose and approximately twenty of them gathered together. They traveled from the Stono Bridge to Ponpon Road gathering strength and numbers as they moved.

Cato and the other enslaved Africans that joined ranks with him were considered to have been Kongolese soldiers captured in battle in central Africa and sold into slavery. They over- whelmed Robert Bathurst and Mr.

Gibbs at the general store in the area of "Hutchenson's Store" along the Stono River on John's Island. There they obtained firearms and powder. They left the heads of these two men on the doorstep as they began their march. They killed the Godfrey family and the Lemys because they did not treat the enslaved well. They continued through what is now Hollywood, South Carolina and continued to proceed south.

Most historians conclude that as they marched and shouted "Liberty! Liberty!", as they were headed to Spanish Florida to claim the freedom that the Spanish king had promised to all negroes that escaped from Carolina, make it to Florida, and convert to Catholicism. They would be manumissed and given arms. Fort Negro was one fortification that became a township for such enslaved Africans, but many believe that this group was headed to Pueblo de Gracia Real de Santa Teresa de Mosé.

Many Gullah/Geechee last names evolved from the professions and sometimes the first names of their foreparents. Interestingly enough, the descendants of Cato took this as their last name.

One such descendant was located during

the Federal Writer's Project's "Works Project Administration" (WPA) interviews. George Cato's interview was scribed by Stiles M. Scruggs as Mr. Cato carried on the African tradition of passing on his family history orally. George Cato is the great great grandson of Cato of the Stono Rebellion. He recalled:

"Yes sah! I sho' does come from dat old stock who had de misfortune to be slaves but who decide to be men, at one and de same time, and I's right proud of it. De first Cato slave we knows 'bout, was plum willin' to lay down his life for de right, as he see it. Dat is pow'ful fine for de Catoes who has come af- ter him. My granddaddy and my daddy tell me plenty 'bout it, while we was livin' in Orangeburg County, not far from where de fightin' took place in de long ago.

My granddaddy was a son of de son of de Stono slave commander. He say his daddy often take him over de route of de rebel slave march, dat time when dere was sho' big trouble all 'bout dat neighborhood. As it come down to me, I thinks de first Cato take a darlin' chance on losin' his life, not so much for his own benefit as it was to help others. He was not lak some slaves, much 'bused by deir masters. My kinfolks not 'bused. Dat why, I reckons, de captain of de slaves was picked by them. Cato was teached how to read and write by the rich master.

How it all start? Dat what I ask but nobody ever tell me how 100 slaves between de Combahee and Edisto rivers come to meet in de woods not far from de Stono River on September 9, 1739. And how they elect a leader, my kinsman, Cato, and late dat day march to Stono town, break in a warehouse, kill two white men in charge, and take all de guns and ammunition they wants. But they do it, wid de start, they turn south and march on.

They work fast, coverin' 15 miles, passin' many fine plantations, and in every single case, stop, and break in de house and kill men, women, and children. Then they take what they want, 'cludin' arms, clothes, liquor and food. Near de Combahee swamp, Lieutenant Governor Bull, drivin' from Beaufort to Charleston, see them and he smell a rat. Befo' he was seen by de army he detour into de big woods and stay 'til de slave rebels pass.

Governor Bull and some planters, between de Combahee and Edisto, ride fast and spread de alarm and it wasn't long 'til de militiamen was on de trail in pursuit of de slave army. When found, many of de slaves was singin' and dancin' and Cap. Cato and some of de the other leaders was cussin' at them sumpin awful. From dat day to dis, no Cato has tasted whiskey, 'less he go 'gainst his daddy's warnin'. Dis war last less than two days but it sho' was pow'fu hot while it last.

I reckons it was hot, 'cause in less than two days, 21 white men, women, and chillun, and 44 Negroes, was slain. My granddaddy say dat in de woods and at Stono, where de war start, dere was more than 100 Negroes in line. When de militia come in sight of them at Combahee swamp, de drinkin' dancin' Negroes scatter in de brush and only 44 stand deir ground.

Commander Cato speak for de crowd. He say: 'We don't lak slavery. We start to jine de Spanish in Florida. We surrender but we not whipped yet and we 'is not converted'. De other 43 say 'Amen.' They was taken, unarmed, and hanged by de militia. Long befo' dis uprisin', de Cato slave wrote passes for slaves and do all he can to send them to freedom. He die for doin' de right, as he see it."

The "slave codes" that were established shortly after the Stono Rebellion took place in 1739 were part of the process of attempting to put an end to these occurrences. The 1740 Negro Act was passed by the Assembly and was used to deprive the African people of any rights. These codes continued to expand over the years to even include that enslaved people in Charleston were not to swear, smoke, walk with a cane, assemble at military parades, or make joyful demonstrations. Banishment from the state, lashes and so on were inflicted if people were found rioting or "insubordinate." "Slave laws" included that if a Black in Charleston was found without a pass after 9 pm, they could be imprisoned or shot if they refused to answer in a satisfactory manner. An enslaved person that ran away or physically struck a white person was whipped, branded, or castrated. The Charleston Workhouse was where the enslaved that were arrested were housed. Runaways and others were placed there daily.

The internal laws were not sufficient to end the quest for freedom. Thus, the enslavers even began banning the importation of Africans from particular regions from coming in since each time there was a major uprising, there appeared to be some of them in the leadership. The thought pattern was that the "domesticated slaves" or those that had been born into enslavement would be more docile. However, the thought of the collective consciousness and the wherewithal of a spirit to seek its own freedom was not taken into account. Therefore, mechanisms to continue to obtain freedom persisted.

In "June 1740 a group of from one hundred and fifty to two hundred Africans in the Goose Creek area 'got together in defiance' of their white overlords. Like the Stono forces, they had no arms and were reportedly planning to break into a Charleston arsenal and then take over the city. As it happened, their plan was betrayed, an ambush was set, and fifty blacks seized. All these were hanged, at the rate of one per day, the aim being, as a white official said, 'to intimidate the other negroes.' Still the struggle continued, and some contemporary observers called the series of risings in South Carolina the 'Gullah War,' identifying elements of an armed conspiracy in Saint Paul's, Saint John's, and Charleston parishes." ("There is a River: The Struggle for Freedom in America" by Vincent Harding 1981 Harcourt Brace & Company p. 35) In

1754 two enslaved females set fire to their master's buildings and he had them burned alive.

Even vicious retaliations against their kinspeople that stood up could not stop the Africans for seeking every opportunity to go into battles for their freedom. The battles that some of the enslaved from the Charleston area went into apparently did not end on North American soil. Some of the German soldiers called the "Hessians" were also people of African descent. Although very few works mention them, in one piece it was stated:

"The drummer John (Jean) Winder of Charleston would appear to have been black if for no other reasons than that most drummers recruited by the Hessians in America were black and that Charleston had a large black population." (p. 291)

"Of the some forty-seven recruits from South Carolina, twenty-eight claimed Charleston as their home, while four claimed Johns Island and one claimed Ponpon, James Island, and Stono Ferry. The Simon who gave his home as Ponpon when enlisting in August 1777 was surely the Wilhelm Simon who joined the same company four years later from a family name."(Jones, Fenwik, "The Black Hessians: Negroes Recruited by the Hessians in South Carolina and Other Colonies" p.292)

No doubt many of these men found their way to Germany by way of the British Army. When what is now called "The American Revolution" began, the skills of Africans were used to build forts and their labor was used for this process as well as to be "body servants" and cooks and such as the battles continued and British blood spilled on the shores of North America. As the fights continued, battalions of enslaved people were put together for them to fight on the side of the colonists as well as the Europeans. The enslaved were promised their freedom in exchange for their service. In 1780 the British landed on John's Island and eventually took command of Charleston. They remained until October of 1782.

"Equaling Virginia in Negro hire, if not surpassing her, was South Carolina. Hired slaves were extensively employed in the boat yards and military hospitals. Their use in defensive operations was illustrated in the early months of the war when the British in June 1776 launched a sea attack against Charleston. But months before the

British arrived, the state capital had set to work erecting fortifications. As early as November 10, 1775, the Provincial Congress had authorized the hiring of 'a sufficient number of Negroes to give all possible dispatch to the completing of the Redoubt erecting upon James Island, to the westward of Fort Johnson. Five weeks later the city authorities began training hired Negroes to extinguish fires and pull down houses, furnishing them with firehooks, axes, and ropes. The Negroes were then ordered to remove the lead. The Council of Safety ordered that colored laborers be employed at all of the town's harbor batteries at the rate of two Negroes to each gun. At Sullivan's Island, key to the city's sea defenses, salaried Negroes did much of the work in putting up the double-walled fort of spongy palmetto logs, with outworks for thirty cannon. As a result of these preparations, one week before His Majesty's forces sailed into Charleston waters, a hundred large guns were poised to greet them. When on June 28, the British finally launched their ill-starred naval attack on the harbor batteries, they were scarcely more amazed by the courage of the American defenders than by the manner in which their forts withstood a ten hour cannonade, absorbing the missiles as if harmlessly sucking them in." (Benjamin Quarles, The Negroes in the American Revolution 1996 U of NC Press Chapel Hill 102-103) Breastworks were even constructed here by the enslaved while others of them were trained to extinguish fires that might erupt in the city.

O'Sullivan was one of the families from which came the name for Sullivan's Island where this fort was built. The fort was named "Fort Sullivan" initially. However, Fort Sullivan was renamed Fort Moultrie after Colonel William Moultrie who was one in command when the British attacked it on June 28, 1776. This was the chief harbor defense until 1947. It was also the location of "Cassina Plantation." Interestingly enough, this was also the chief entry point of finances as Africans continued to come in and be placed in the "pest houses" just outside the fortress.

Relations between Negroes and the British forces in occupation of Charleston did not always turn upon labor service. "On an evening in January 1782, a group of officers put aside the cares of the day to attend an 'Ethiopian Ball,' whose managers were three 'Negro Wenches assuming their

Mistress's names.' The female slaves invited to the affair had been "dressed up in taste, with the richest silks, and the false rolls in their heads," the expenses borne by their officers escorts. 'This Ball was held at a very capital private House in Charlestown," wrote an indignant American prisoner, "and the Supper cost not less than £80 Sterling, and these tyrants danced with these Slaves until four o'clock in the morning.'

Despite the indignation of an American patriot, the infrequency of such social notes from Charleston serves but to underscore the Negro's labor contribution to the British armies in the South Carolina theatre. This contribution is cogently illustrated in two lines from an English officer at Camden to General Cornwallis: 'Your lordship will not be Surprised that our works are not in greater forwardness. The Negroes took the Small Pox, Deserted, Many Died.'

***In the final campaigns of the war the British continued to employ Negroes on a large scale. Blacks accompanied the moving army as Cornwallis departed Charleston in the winter of 1781 and moved northward to meet his destiny at Yorktown." (Quarles, Revolution 140)

"From British headquarters at Charleston in March 1782, General Alexander Leslie ordered a cavalry detail to proceed to Daniel's Island to collect slaves making it known to them that if they behaved with fidelity they might depend upon the generosity of the English. A week later the officer in charge of the expedition reported that although he had induced 100 blacks to join him, the number was less than expected because the American masters had 'taken the precaution of sending their most valuable slaves across the River.' "(Quarles Revolution 127)

These who attempted to keep the "most valuable" across creeks must have had insight into realizing that many that were not held back would make passages back across the ocean. During the American Revolution, Brigadier General Samuel Birch was given a command to create a process to ascertain which Blacks fought for the crown. The ones that did were free to depart with the fleet when it returned to England. At the end if 1700s there were 775 free colored people in Charleston, SC.

Documenting the people of African descent was an on-going practice. A man named Birch issued certificates and recorded the names of those to whom they were issued. The book in which Birch recorded the names of the people became known as "the Book of Negroes." In this was an entry concerning Boston King who had been owned by Richard Waring of Charleston, SC. King went to Charleston and when the British surrendered that city, he was taken to New York on one of the warships. There he did odd jobs and also married Violet who was of African and Native American descent from Wilmington, North Carolina. King began piloting a boat, but got caught and sold back into slavery in New Jersey. He made it back to Violet. They boarded L'Abondance in the New York Harbor along with the Black Brigade which was a group of escaped and free blacks who had fought for the British during the Revolutionary War.

There were approximately 4000 of them that made their way to freedom. The 408 passengers on the ship left from New York and went to Port Roseway in Nova Scotia. They formed the community of Birchtown there. King became an evangelist and eventually set sail to Sierra Leone on a Sierra Leone Company ship.

The Africans that remained in Charleston were soon to not only be faced with continued strengthening of abuses from those that they called "massa," but also from a board of police that was established. "The Board [of Police] was concerned not only with the care of the poor but also with that other dependent element in eighteenth-century Charles Town society, the Negro. Considerable embarrassment was caused the British forces by those slaves who had deserted their masters and had attempted to join the British army, presumably in the hope of thereby attain- ing their freedom. Lord Cornwallis hoped that some way could be worked out to persuade the Negroes to return to their masters and, at the same time, to persuade the masters not to punish those slaves who had defected to the British. At the Board's suggestion, three men were appointed to supervise the return of these runaway slaves to their rightful owners. These three gentlemen were to purchase rice to feed their charges and to keep them employed, preferably on some public project, until such time as they could be returned to their masters. This effort to return the defected slaves must be carried through with some success; for, in September 1780, the commandant informed the intendants of police that a hundred able bodied Negroes were needed for a fortnight 'to repair some of the works and Lines about the Town.' The Board advised the commandant to impress the required slaves from certain stipulated plantations. In November 1780, the Board, in response to an application from Major Moncrief, the chief engineer, again had to resort to the impressment of three hundred Negroes to 'repair Fortifications and for other Works in Charles Town'.

Control of the conduct of the Negroes was also a problem. With this in mind, the intendants of the police recommended that the commandant employ troops to deal with the insurrectional behavior of the slaves on the plantations. The unruly conduct of Negroes and other 'disorderly Persons' in the punch houses and dram shops in the city prompted the Board to pass stricter regulations concerning licenses for 'houses of public entertainment' and for the sale of liquor.

Also in respect to the Negro, the Board of Police endeavored to enforce the proclamation of the commandant designed to prevent the illegal exportation of Negroes. This proclamation required a ship captain to post a bond promising to comply with the regulations concerning the exportation of Negroes set up under the applicable acts of Assembly of the province." (McCowen p.38-39)

Exportation and importation regulations regarding the sale of "negroes" was already in place. However, these two words would now take on new restrictions as the exportation laws took hold and importation and immigration laws were shaped. Many of the restrictions were coming out of the fears that were being carried by those that were enslaving the Africans.

In August 1793 the lieutenant governor of Virginia warned that a slave revolt of immigrants from St. Domingue was going to attempt to engulf South Carolina as of October 13th. The French brig Maria did bring a group of refugees into Charleston at the beginning of October. As the Haitian Revolution became more ignited in July 1793, more refugees including Jacques Delaire came to Charleston. The French Popular Society was also formed in Charleston in 1792. In addition Gullah/Geechees no doubt heard of the Haitian Independence that came in 1804 and the freedom of the Dominican Republic that came in 1844. They used these as information and inspiration for their plans for free- dom.

To further attempt to thwart assistance with plans of freedom for the Africans, in 1795 the South Carolina Legislature prohibited the immigration of foreign free colored people because they feared uprisings. Many of the previously enslaved had become a part of the free population already. Thus, in 1820 the Legislature tried to put in a law prohibiting masters from manumissing slaves.

Just as there had to be a gathering of Gullah/Geechees from different walks of life to pull together the Gullah/Geechee Nation in the year 2000, there was a pulling together of the enslaved and the free during the many years of enslavement. One of the greatest opportunities for connection happened in the praise houses and later in the churches.

As evangelism started to sweep the eastern seaboard of North America, it did not pass by the hearts or minds of the people of African descent. Africans had continued to gather on their own in their own forms of worship since their enslavement.

The "slave codes" and fears of meetings to plan uprisings began to take tolls on large gatherings. However, prostyletizers of the time felt that the Africans and those enslaving them needed to be reached. They did not take into account that Jesus had been born on the same continent that they had descended from because they had another concept of Christianity to propagate. As they convinced or converted some enslavers, praise houses were built on some plantations. In areas of the townships and large parishes, churches were built often with "slave galleries" upstairs. However, the methods and the messages of these gatherings were not the same as that which the Africans connected to on their own.

The difference in the process of spiritual presentations and worship services no doubt were a part of the reason that Wesleyan Methodism had a difficult time taking hold. However, the greater part had to do with the messengers, Joseph Philmoore and George Whitefield.

Philmoore came to Charleston in 1773. Thirty-three years earlier George Whitefield had tried to bring this doctrine to the region. They both found this area to be hostile toward them given that their beliefs spoke against slavery. In 1785 they were finally able to establish a church when Francis Asbury who had organized the Methodist Episcopal church in America came to Charleston and had Henry Willis and Jesse Lee work with him. The initial church had 35 whites and 23 "colored" in it. They first met at the Baptist meeting house until that was disrupted and then they continued to seek buildings until they erected the Cumberland Street Church.

In 1794, William Hammett was in charge of the Charleston Methodist Church. He was criticized for his "slaveholding." John Phillips who had lead the accusations against Hammett wrote an appeal to the Charleston people denouncing slavery. Most likely armed with this, people accused Hammett of giving enslaved people passes that allowed them to go about the town day and night. As a result, he was put out of the pulpit.

This denomination at first wanted all members to manumit the enslaved and compensate them for labor, but they backed down on this. Even though they let up on this issue that did not make them accepted. Members got arrested for openly fraternizing with whites after going to services together. In 1793, the Charleston church had 280 blacks and 65 whites.

By 1800 there was only one Methodist church south of Charleston located on Edisto Island. By 1818 Edisto Island Baptist Church was also established there. Hephzibah Jenkins Townsend is the true mother of this church in that she is credited with leading the movement to have the church fully turned over to the Gullah/Geechees of that island just after the Civil War. There is a monument to her memory outside of the church while the slave gallery that lines the walls of the nave of the church on its interior serve as a monument to the things that the people pulled together to overcome.

"Beginning in 1815, free blacks and slaves had joined together in an unprecedented act of religious self-determination. When the white Methodist Church cancelled certain privileges for blacks within its congregations, the blacks communicated with the newly organized African Methodist Episcopal Church in Philadelphia. They sent two representatives to be ordained as ministers, and finally established their own separate church.

Most of the 'class leaders,' or deacons, resigned from the white-dominated Methodist Church; and almost 5,000 blacks, three-quarters of the black membership, transferred their allegiance to the new African Church." (Starobin, Robert S. "Denmark Vesey: the Slave Conspiracy of 1822 p. 2)

"In Charleston, South Carolina, the number of slaves and free blacks in the Methodist society totaled about four thousand in 1815. Up to that year the black members had been allowed their own separate quarterly conference, with their own preachers and class leaders in charge of financial and disciplinary affairs. Upon the discovery of some financial irregularities, the white preacher in charge ordered the black officers to hand over all collections to the stewards and to conduct church trials only in his presence. The black leaders resented this intrusion, and when their separate quarterly conference was abolished, the black membership began to move in secret to form their own church. Two members of the African society, including Morris Brown, were sent to Philadelphia, where they were ordained by Bishop Richard Allen and commissioned to return to Charleston to organize an A.M.E. [African Methodist Episcopal] church...In 1822 the African Church was suppressed by civil authorities after the discovery of the Vesey plot. Even the church building was ordered demolished. Morris Brown was spirited North and separate African Methodism was not revived until A.M.E. missionaries returned to Charleston after the war." (Rabbatou p. 204-205)

During the early years of the AME church in Charleston, the members lived out persecutions that resembled those that would have been dictated by Saul himself. On December 3, 1817 the Charleston city guard invaded the church and arrested 469 blacks on charges of disorderly conduct. The members did all that they could to conduct their worship with things being done "decently and in order." In 1818 they wrote a petition to the South Carolina House of Representatives that read:

"The free persons of colour attached to the African Methodist Episcopal Church in Charleston called Zion, have erected a house of worship at Hampstead on Charleston Neck at the corner of Hanover and Reid Streets. Petitioners request to open said building for the purpose of Divine worship from the rising of the sun until the going down of the sun."

The petition was denied and on the first Sunday in June 1818, the Charleston guard raided the church again. This time they arrested 150 people, mostly ministers, elders, and class leaders for violations of city ordinances. They were either fined $5, whipped with ten lashes, or put in prison. Most took prison in order to continue with their congregation.

"Black Methodists had enjoyed an independent quarterly conference in the early 1800s. They had control of their own collections from which they distributed to needy members of their community, and they maintained internal jurisdiction over the church trial of black members. Although many facets of black life contributed to seeds of discontent, the loss of this control over their religious life prompted visible action. White Methodists first moved against the black Methodists contacted the Philadelphia AME Church, sending two representatives, Morris Brown and Henry Drayton, to be ordained for pastorates. Disputes over custody of a black burial ground gave the black secessionists their immediate pretext for withdrawal from the white organization. Led by Morris Brown, most of the black deacons, called class leaders, and over four-fifths of the

6,000 black worshipers removed their membership from the three white Methodist churches. This was clearly an illegal act and a move of group assertion, precipitating protests from white church leadership and repression from the authorities. In 1817 blacks organized the Charleston African Association, establishing several churches out of their massive members, one on Anson Street, one on Cow Alley, and one in Hampstead, the latter being most closely linked to the rebellion attempt. In December 1817, when blacks began holding worship, 469 were arrested for disorderly conduct. In 1818 the city guard arrested 140 blacks from the Hampstead Church including Morris Brown. The black Methodists were charged with instructing slaves without the presence of whites. 'Bishop' Brown and four ministers were sentenced to serve either a month in jail or banishment from the state. Brown chose jail. Eight other black ministers were sentenced to floggings, fines, and banishments." (Creel p. 149) Brown was a prosperous shoemaker who purchased enslaved people in order to manumit them before laws prohibited this.

"To preserve the 'domestic tranquility' of the state, whites moved against the black community again in 1820. An act passed that year forbade any more free blacks from entering the state; if freedmen left the state, they were forbidden to return. Considering the African Methodists' journey to Pennsylvania, the new law was a direct attack on the religious integrity of all blacks. To discourage further entry of free blacks into the state, those not born in South Carolina or residents of less than five years were subject to a stiff, fifty-dollar-a-year tax. Manumission of slaves was also severely proscribed, and licenses were now required of blacks for certain occupations to reduce competition with whites. Altogether, Charleston blacks-both free and slave-found themselves under considerable pressure." (p. 2 Starobin, Robert S. "Denmark Vesey: the Slave Conspiracy of 1822 Prentice-Hall Inc., Englewood Cliffs NJ)

"A majority of the slaves executed for conspiring to revolt in Charleston, South Carolina, in 1822 were members of the city's African Methodist Church. Two of the conspirators were class leaders, and several witnesses implicated Morris Brown, pastor of the church and later assistant bishop to Richard Allen." (Rabbateuo p. 163) As a result of these allegations the church was closed by whites.

"The African Methodist Episcopal Church, dormant in South Carolina from 1822 until 1865 because of while hostility, was re-organized in the latter year by a group under the leadership of Bishop Daniel Alexander Payne, who had been exiled from his native Charleston for thirty years. Under the leadership of energetic ministers, the most successful of who was Richard Harvey Cain, the African Methodists had by the end of Reconstruction established themselves as the second largest Negro denomination in the state. The Emmanuel Church in Charleston, organized by Cain, was the leading church of this denomination, with a membership in 1883 of 3878." (p. 190, Tindall, George Brown, "South Carolina Negroes 1877-1900)

Before this dormant period, the eyes of those that had become a part of this congregation had their eyes opened and focused on freedom. One of Denmark Vesey's comrades stated "we were deprived of our rights and privileges by the white people and that our Church [Hamstead] was shut up so that we could not use it, and that it was high time for us to seek for our rights, and that we were fully able to conquer the whites if we were only unanimous and courageous, as the Santo Domingo people were." This statement had to have struck a chord with Vesey and it started a tune that would play for generations.

"Télemaque" who came to be known as "Denmark Vesey" had been born in Saint Thomas and was enslaved there. He won $1500 in a lottery on East Bay Street when he got there and purchased his own freedom and then obtained a home for himself. "By 1817 Vesey had evidently decided that the only new life he desired was a struggle for the freedom of his people. One of his companions said that Vesey often rebuked any of his friends who offered the customary black gesture of bowing to a white person on the street. Vesey claimed that 'all men were born equal, and that he was surprised that anyone would degrade himself by such conduct; that he would never cringe to whites, nor ought any who had feelings of a man.' Such feelings were not uncommon in the black community, and were often expressed within its confines. It was not common, however, to act on them publicly or urge others to do the same. Denmark Vesey did both, and plunged forthrightly into the stream of black radicalism." (Harding, "There is a River: The Struggle for Freedom in

America" p.67)

Gullah Jack worked with Vesey to finally encourage others to take the same plunge. "By December of 1821 Vesey was beginning to talk about direct action. His expressions of dissatisfaction began to hint at an objective. Negroes in Charleston, he said, were living such an abominable life and their situation was so bad that he did not know how they could endure it. The time was at hand when they should not be slaves of damn white rascals any longer but should fight for liberty. After all, he observed, the ability of Negroes to fight had been proved at the Battle of New Orleans (in 1814) where black men had been in the line and had helped to hold the city.

With the voicing of such sentiments, the die was cast. Once such a daring goal as a fight for freedom was communicated to other Negroes without attracting the lightning of white retribution, it became easier to take the next steps-to choose lieutenants for the enterprise and to begin making concrete plans. By winter of 1821-22 Vesey, having demonstrated his boldness and his gift for argument, had acquired a reputation with and considerable influence over Negroes of Charleston.

Some black acquaintances feared him, some admired him, all respected him. As a man of obvious intelligence and ability, as a domineering personality who scorned any sign of weakness among his fellows, as a Negro who was recognized as a man of capacity even among whites, Vesey naturally could sway Negroes of lesser stature. This was to help him in enlisting recruits.

Before assembling an army of followers, however, Vesey had to select able lieutenants. He chose well, with a view not only to the character of his aides, but to the strategic usefulness of their connections in the community. His first two deputies were Ned and Rolla Bennett, confidential servants of Thomas Bennett, the governor of South Carolina." (Lofton p. 134-135) After them came Jack Purcell who was a zealous promoter of the effort. Peter Poyas, who was a ship carpenter who could write extremely well and was trusted by his master came next. James Poyas was also a "trusted servant" and a cautious planner. James Poyas lived at 49 Kings Street and at a place on the Cooper River. He also operated a shipyard at 35 South Bay.

Just after Christmas of 1821, Gullah Jack was recruited. He had escaped from the plantation of Zephaniah Kingsley in Florida during a raid. Kingsley had purchased Gullah Jack in Zinguebar which could possibly be today's "Zanzibar." However, Gullah Jack was a native of M'Coolay Moreema and he knew a language that was spoken from one coast of Africa to another. This was no doubt a predecessor of what has come to be called "Gullah" or "Gullah/Geechee" in North America. Numerous linguists feel that the trade language that Africans had on the continent was what continued as the Gullah language once the Africans that were enslaved on the Sea Islands remained in isolation and the language with its adoption of some English words into its vocabulary solidified. This language which is a "code of the spirit" no doubt served to easily connect Gullah Jack with the people that were in Charleston and to whom he would need to communicate what it was time for them to do together.

Gullah Jack was now on the Paul Pritchard shipyard. Pritchard stayed at 6 Hassell Street and had the shipyard at Gadsden's Wharf. On his own time, Gullah Jack led the *Gullah Society."* Many believe that his followers saw him as a conjurer with great influence and discipline.

"Monday, a slave of John Gell, was the last member of the group of five principal officers engaged by Vesey. A man in the prime of his life, Monday was regarded by white men who observed him as intelligent, steady, and dependable. Though he was Ebo [or Egbo] in origin, a member of one of the tribes of the lower Niger, he had by 1822 been in the United States fifteen or twenty years. His master being the operator of a lively stable- at 127 Church Street-Monday was a harness maker, and an excellent one. He pursued his craft in a shop on Meeting Street. Since his time and a share of his earnings were at his own disposal, his status was above the common level of slavery." (Lofton p. 136)

The word of meetings continued to spread as the planning went on. Some meetings were held at Vesey's home at Bull and Smith, Monday Gell's shop, and Bulkley's farm on Charleston Neck. The Bible as well as newspaper accounts of the stand in Haiti were often read as mechanisms of justification for this plan and inspiration for those that would carry it out.

Drunks and babblers were excluded from being allowed to join the ranks. People with skills such as Mingo Harth, a

Mandingo mechanic and Tom Russell, a blacksmith, were central to the force. Gullah Jack did warn Vesey not to tell any mulattos of their plans. Many of them had their own personal interest to protect by aiding and abedding the system of enslavement. The likelihood of this probably never was a thought in Vesey's mind since he knew what freedom felt like and thought that it was just for all to have it. Therefore, he told some of the wrong men that Sunday July 14th would be the day that some seven sets of different forces would come from the islands and various areas of the peninsula and take up the arms and ammunition that had already been prepared and placed with masks and other necessary items around the area. Even though the plot was well designed and strategically planned, "the conspirators never had an opportunity to carry out their plot due to the timely intervention of a slave, Peter Devany Prioleau, who, on the advice of his friend, William Pencil, a free black, informed his master who in turn notified white authorities." (Before Freedom Came 140) Devany was the fifty-five year old enslaved by John C. Prioleau.

Two men named William were also part of the informants. William who was enslaved by J and D. Paul were house "slaves." William Pencil was a tinplate worker. William Paul was kept in solitary confinement for nine days until he incriminated the others. Another informant was a leader in the African church named George who was enslaved by the Wilsons.

Gullah Jack took up the leadership and the plot was still to be carried out even after Vesey had been taken into custody. It is documented that they were going to move the date to June 16th in order to make sure that those that had gotten the other date would be caught off guard. However, on July 5th, the plan had not taken place and Gullah Jack was found and also taken into custody. This betrayal lead to the hanging of Denmark Vesey, Gullah Jack, and many others publicly on the peninsula after short trials. July 26 was the day of a mass execution of those that had worked with the leaders. It was held on King Street. Those that had "turned states evidence" including Charles Drayton, Monday Gell, and Harry Haig were beaten or simply deported and exiled.

The continued murdering of Africans that attempted to hold on to their God given birthright of freedom was expected to deter all other African people from their attempts at the same. However, it did not work. One person that was born free and felt that what he had should also be shared was the AME Bishop Payne. He was born of free Black parents in Charleston, South Carolina. In 1828, at age seventeen he established his own school which was later closed due to state laws saying that educating blacks was a crime. He was ran out of Charleston by whites in 1835. He then spent his time in seminary and establishing schools for blacks. In 1852 he was elected bishop. In 1865 he sailed into Charleston Harbor along with some missionaries and established the South Carolina Conference of the AME Church. Thus, embarking on establishing a number of churches in the south.

Many of the needs of the entire person were attended to in spiritual sacred spaces. "In the 1830s and 1840s, some southern ministers became increasingly concerned with what they perceived as the neglect of the spiritual needs of the slave population. The plantation missionary movement they advocated was hailed all over the South but was most actively pursued in the lowcountry of South Carolina and Georgia. Given the fact that three-fourths of the population in this area were slaves, the coastal plantations were considered an opportune target for religious reform. Consequently it is in the lowcountry that buildings constructed explicitly for slave worship were most commonplace." (Vlach, John Michael, Back to the Big House: The Architecture of Plantation Slavery p. 148)

The people that took to these buildings became extremely devoted to these spaces. In Mount Pleasant, Thomas Pickney was the sexton of the Presbyterian Church who was able to write a synopsis of each sermon as he sat in the "slave gallery" upstairs. He was a licensed preacher that could then go back and deliver the exact same sermon with the same inflections. St. Andrew's Episcopal Church had Edmund Robinson as the sexton. He lived in the Harleston yard.

In Charleston, when the Calvary Episcopal Church for Negroes was built in 1849. It was considered by some to be a threat to slavery. Thus, a mob intended to tear it down after a Negro revolt at a work house. In spite of the constant threats to the church buildings and members, the hearts of the members stayed consistent.

The AME Church is still prominent in Charleston County, South Carolina, but so is the "fear of black radicalism." It has continued to exist in the City of Charleston as evidenced by the outrage express by citizens when Mayor Joseph P. Riley had a painting of Denmark Vesey hung in the Gaillard Auditorium and also through the fact that a group of citizens have tried for years to place a monument to Denmark Vesey in Marion Square Park (given its historic location and proximity to Emmanuel AME Church) have continually been denied that opportunity. It has been reported that this park is owned by two Anglo "militia groups." They will not allow such a monument to be erected within the park that all visitors to historic downtown Charleston pass.

"The passions loosed by the abortive Denmark Vesey insurrection in 1822 precipitated the passage of various restrictive laws against slaves and free Negroes, in particular, the first of the Negro Seamen Acts. Designed to prevent the contamination of the local slave population with dangerous ideas, the act required the arrest and imprisonment of all Negro seamen as long as their ships remained in port. In the first test of the law United

States Supreme Court Justice William Johnson pointedly noted that Petrigru as the Attorney General of the state had not appeared to defend the statute but that the enforcement of the law had been pressed by a private organization. Petigru believed, then as later, that this enactment infringed the federal government's constitutional power over interstate and foreign commerce and was an unconscionable attempt to deprive free men of liberty." (Tyler p. 274)

This statement was good, but yet "two acts passed during the period that deserve particular attention. As a result of the great Vesey slave conspiracy in Charleston in 1822 a great deal of repressive and discriminatory legislation was enacted. Much of this was directed particularly against "free Negroes" some of whom had played important parts in the event, the leader, himself, of course, having been free.

By an act of December 21, 1822 South Carolina established an armed guard, not to exceed one hundred and fifty men, for the city of Charleston. The expenses for this guard were to be defrayed by a tax of ten dollars upon every free male Negro mechanic, plus a tax of ten dollars upon every house owned or occupied by Negroes-a heavy burden indeed.

Also to be noted is the fact that in 1833, again following excitement consequent upon the revolts and plots of 1831-32, South Carolina enacted a law permitting the sale into forced labor for one year of Negroes who failed to pay their poll tax, though whether this was ever enforced is not clear. Certainly, a leading Carolina jurist, writing in 1848, expressed grave doubts as to the constitutionality of the statute." (Journal of Negro History Volume 31/1946-SC Poll Tax by Herbert Aptheker p.137-138)

Also, in December of 1822, "An Act for the Better Regulation and Government of Free Negroes and Persons of Color" was passed by the South Carolina Legislature. It required every free man of color to have a white guardian in the district where he or she resided. Anyone who did not obtain a guardian was to be sold as a slave with one-half the proceeds going to the informer and the other half to the state. These people were then listed in the Charleston Free Negro Tax Books that were held at the city treasurer's office. "Free blacks, after the 1830s, secured the freedom of many of their kin in this way, designating a white guardian in a deed of trust.

In the eyes of the law, however, they were still slaves, and their offspring were slaves as well. During the 1850s, authorities in South Carolina decided to enforce the 1822 state law prohibiting manumissions. Therefore, any black unable to prove manumission prior to that date was a slave, regardless of any deed of trust or other arrangement. The crackdown was especially hard on Charleston's free blacks since, as one white observed in 1848, there were 'evasions [of the 1822 law] without number.' In connection with the renewed enforcement of an 1820s law requiring slaves to wear badges in order to obtain work, the strictures posed a dilemma for the city's blacks. To work without a badge one had to prove freedom—either the black or his mother or grandmother (since freedom descended from the mother's line) had to have been manumitted prior to 1822 and possess the papers to prove it. If the authorities arrested a black without a badge and the individual could not prove his or her freedom, the penalty was typically appropriation of the black and the black's property by the city. But to buy a badge was an admission that one was not, in fact, a free black, but a slave. Charleston's officials swooped into action during the spring of 1860, a time of heightened sectional tension and growing political power among white workingmen (1860 was the first time in the city's history that census takers had recorded a white majority). Arrests of 'slaves' working without badges increased from zero in March to twenty-seven in April and up to ninety-three in August. In a sense, the sweep was an attempt to re-enslave free blacks." (Before Freedom Came 150)

"Charleston's free Afro-American population never exceeded eight per cent and was generally about six per cent of the city's total." ("Black Charlestonians" p. 305) This percentage probably remained low due to the constant changes in the law regarding the status of the people of African descent. This caused many of them to begin to seek other means of recourse outside of Charleston.

"Because of their tenuous status, Charleston's free Afro-Americans became increasingly interested in emigrating to Liberia. They displayed this trend much earlier than their counterparts in New Orleans. In 1832, approximately fifty Charleston free Afro-American families prepared to leave the city. They were well-educated, owned property, and were skilled. They assembled together and agreed unanimously that emigration was their best alternative, with the hope that they could contribute positively to the 'land of their fathers.' Several months later a free Afro-American Charlestonian wrote to the African Repository, journal of the American Colonization Society which had fostered emigration to Liberia since its inception in 1817. He explained that prejudice against color of Afro-Americans barred their mental improvement in particular and that European immigrants had settled in Charleston and prospered, while Afro-Americans languished. One of the major reasons for their reluctance to emigrate, he guessed, was the Liberians' darker complexion. He reminded them that this was no impediment for the many prominent white men and women who had settled in Africa. Afro-Americans could be free citizens in Liberia, he promised, and would not have to associate with any-one against their wishes. He urged them to leave with family and friends and to thereby continued their own customs and habits. The primary reason for them to quit Charleston was that they would have no superiors in Liberia, where they could realize freedom, education, and prosperity.

Thomas C Brown, a Charleston free Afro-American, lived in Liberia for fourteen months from 1833 to 1834. A committee of the American Anti-Slavery Society in New York City examined him on his experience abroad when he returned to this country. Born in Charleston around 1800, he had been a carpenter with three thousand dollars in real estate. He could trace his ancestry in South Carolina for four generations. With his wife, three children, his mother, brother, and two sisters, he had gone to Liberia to better himself and to raise his family without the weight of racial prejudice. He soon lost his two children, his brother and a sister to the area's climate. He had a wholesale store, but became disappointed and left Liberia because of his health and inability to make a good living. In concluding his testimony, Brown warned that free Afro-Americans would not voluntarily go to Liberia if they knew the real situation there." (Powers p.307-308)

Jehu Jones Sr. was one of many that wanted to go to Liberia. "From 1832 to

1860, four hundred and eighty-three Afro-Americans left Charleston for Liberia. William E Berry, also a Humane Brotherhood man, sought to change his life chances by going to Haiti." (Powers p. 309)

"Retired Republican probate judge, H. N. "Bouey was to be an important figure in the organization of the effort to carry our a mass exodus. In the spring of 1877 he was selected as a juror in the United States District Court in Charleston, and there met George Curtis, another juror, native of British Guiana (sic) and resident of Beaufort, who was also full of the spirit of emigration. The two men sought out the Reverend B. F. Porter, pastor of Morris Brown AME Church, who was very enthusiastic about the idea. By chance, Professor J. C. Hazeley, a native African, was in Charleston at the same time to deliver lectures on the advantages of emigration. On the fourth of July a celebration was held at Morris Brown Church at which a number of addresses were delivered on behalf of emigration. On July 26 a mass meeting was called to celebrate the thirtieth anniversary of the Liberian Declaration of Independence. A parade culminated at the Mall where four thousand Negroes gathered to hear

George Curtis read the Liberian Declaration of Independence and the Reverend B. F. Porter deliver a twenty minute address in favor of the exodus. A proposition made by Porter for the formation of a stock company with thirty thousand shares of stock at $10 a share 'met with much evident favor,' and the Liberian Exodus Joint Stock Steamship Company with B. F. Porter as president and H. N. Bouey as secretary was soon after organized." (p. 155-156, Tindall, George Brown, "South Carolina Negroes 1877-1900 University of South Carolina Press)

The statewide enthusiasm about the project caused upheaval amongst the Anglos and rumors were spread in order to cause major opposition to it. It was stated that the *American Colonization Society* was paying J. C. Hazeley $200 per month to get the cheap labor force of the "Negroes" to leave. The Anglos could not allow this because their businesses would be ruined. Rumors of this being a tactic to actually enslaved the "Negroes" in Cuba was used to scare people from joining the movement and also financial incentives were given in the form of drafts that could only be used in the counties were the people already were.

Martin R. Delany was brought in to the movement to assist the newspapers and leaders with keeping the momentum of the project going. Delany could speak to the reality of life in Africa because he had been traveling there as a part of a project to colonize Niger with "Negroes from the United States." The churches were initially opposed to the movement for fear of losing their members as well. However, they slowly came to be a part of the movement.

In January of 1878 many groups of people came to Charleston because they heard that the ships were ready to depart. However, there were none. The officers of the exodus association worked with them to get jobs in the phosphate mines.

In order to try and quickly rectify the situation, on March 18th the *Azor* arrived from Boston to the port of Charleston. It had been selected by B. F. Porter and paid for with $6000 made from sale of stocks. The captain estimated a twenty-five day trip to Monrovia with the passengers split between 19 berths for cabins and 140 berths for steering passengers. On the 21st of March, the ladies of the *St. Joseph's Union* presented Martin R. Delany with the flag of Liberia for the journey. This was part of a 5000 person spiritual service at *White Point Garden* over which Reverend Henry M. Turner presided.

One month after the celebration 206 passengers left another 175 behind on the shore. Due to the weight of goods on the ship, they could not take any more people. Those that remained went to a plantation that was purchased by the association along the Wando River. The emigrants organized the African Methodist Episcopal Church and the Shiloh Baptist Church.

23 people passed away on the journey due to fever. There was not doctor on board even though there should have been by law. There was not enough water and the food supply was poor and not enough for all on board. Thus, what was meant to assist them when they got to Liberia, were all utilized on the crossing. The people that got to Liberia found that the dollar value on the receipts for their provisions did not match the value of what they were issued and things such as the grist mill that they were to use were not in existence.

When the ship stopped in Sierra Leone, additional charges were added to the journey for supplies, pilotage, and towage that had to be done by a British steamer called *"Senegal."* These bills ended up financially breaking the association. Thus, in January 1879 a journey for passengers willing to pay $40-65 per person was to be charged in order to recover.

They were to leave on February 20, but this did not happen. The *Azor* was then a central component of a court case. Although the association tried to raise funds to keep the ship, it was sold at an auction by order of the court in November of that year. Edward Willis purchased it with an agreement that the association would repurchase it from him. However, Rogers sold it to a company in Boston long before the contract with the association came due. So, when they presented the funds to retrieve the ship, it had long since left Charleston headed north from whence it had come.

Even with all of the problems associated with this effort, success did come to those that settle in Liberia after some time. "In 1890 it was reported that Charleston had furnished to Liberia some of its most prominent citizens. C. L. Parsons, Chief Justice of the Liberian Supreme

Court, was a native of Charleston. Clement Irons, another native of Charleston, had built the first steamship constructed in Liberia. It had been launched on the St. Paul's River in December 1888. In 1891 the Reverend David Frazier, an emigrant from South Carolina, was elected to the Liberian Senate. He had opened a coffee farm with twenty thousand trees and was hoping to have thirty thousand the following year." (Tindall p. 167)

No doubt these men and the women that accompanied them on their migration back to the Motherland thought that even an unknown place had to be better than what they were currently faced with. The continued fervor toward re-enslavement of the free Africans/Gullah/Geechees was clearly expressed in the fact that:

"Antebellum southern society placed considerable emphasis on show; a fine house, expensive appointments, and fashionable clothes helped to define the status of a lady or gentleman. Clothing, in other words, was a reflection of an individual's place in society. It was inconceivable and irritating to some that those with the least status-African Americans-should presume to be something they were not-full and equal citizens of southern urban society...Coming in the wake of the Vesey conspiracy, such violations of etiquette were difficult to swallow. Soon, a Charleston grand jury proposed requiring blacks to dress 'only in coarse stuffs' because 'every distinction should be created between the whites and the negroes, calculated to make the latter feel the superiority of the former.' The proposal went nowhere, although dress codes for blacks continued to be a contentious issue among some whites, ostensibly because of his flashy attire." (Before Freedom Came 142)

To wear "coarse stuffs" was a sign of being enslaved. The "chattel" was not at liberty to dress in fine garments unless these had been presented as hand me downs from massa or missus. This was no doubt adding insult to injury for those that had been born free and now could possibly be enslaved or to those that had fought hard to buy their way out of bondage.

"Although direct protest by urban blacks was obviously limited during the 1850s, they did not entirely leave their defense to wavering white protectors or owners... As the Charleston debacle unfolded in 1859 and

1860, free blacks there resorted to several tactics. They challenged police sent to enforce regulations (and from at least one account, the police retreated), and they lobbied influential whites, particularly their customers who depended upon their labor. After these strategies proved of limited effectiveness, many chose another option-migration, even though for some that meant the forced sale of property.

They left for the North, Philadelphia or Boston, for example, some for Haiti and some to other cities in the South where they had friends or relatives. A few stayed. Between August and November 1860, more than seven hundred free blacks left Charleston. The Philadelphia correspondent of the New York Tribune filed the following report:

All have been driven suddenly out of employments by which they gained a living, and are now seeking, under great disadvantages, to begin life anew. Many had acquired real estate and other property, but in the haste to get away were compelled to sell at great loss, while of what they leave behind unsold, they fully expect to be cheated. Some leave relations behind them-an old mother, a decrepid [sic] father-whom they are unable to bring away. Some have brought with them their copper badges, which read thus: Charleston, 1860, Servant, 1243.

This was obviously the most unsatisfactory option of all: leaving one's home, where one had lived and worked and had shared fellowship for generations. The new destination was not likely to afford better opportunities. To be black in America, regardless of latitude, meant to be less than free." (Before Freedom Came 153) Those that went to Philadelphia found this to be true. They did not have to walk around with passes as they had in Charleston, but they were not allowed entry to museums and such. There is no freedom with limitations on movement.

This feeling has been shared by many people of African descent since America was established. This feeling did not stop the realities of exploitation that continued to be put into operation in order to keep impressing this reality on the minds of the people. More oft than not, when the enslavement could not be easily done physically, it was done financially. This financial bondage has often come in the form of taxations. Such as was the case in 1860 when free persons of color were required to pay a state capitation tax assessed by the city council.

Ellisons, Johnsons, Lees, Mathews, and Dereefs were among the free families that stayed in spite of the fact that they could possibly never see their family members that left again. Laws were put in place to prohibit the return of blacks that had left. Those that stayed were being economically challenged as less affluent whites began to seek as many legal means as possible to oppress them. This was evidenced by the fact that:

"Encouraged, white workingmen pressed their case further with the state legislature. They elected two of their own in 1859, James M Eason and Henry T. Peake. In 1860, they introduced a bill to prevent free blacks from engaging in any arsenal occupations, a measure sure to deal a severe blow to Charleston's free black population. The bill failed, but the two mechanics were undeterred and introduced an even more damaging bill to enslave all free blacks living within the state by 1 January 1862. The objective was to induce free blacks to leave the state- thereby eliminating a work force competitor. That bill also failed. Soon thereafter, the firing on Fort Sumter and the war overcame efforts to remove blacks from the labor force." (Before Freedom Came 152)

The labor force would have been alright to remain in tact if it consisted of "free labor" with the Africans being enslaved and the Anglos reaping the financial benefit. However, no other system would do in the minds of many including the men that attempted to put forth the failed bills.

In 1860, the enslaved that worked in Charleston were required to have a badge that their owners purchased annually. The cost of the badges depended on the type of trade that the person had. A handicraft tradesmen's badge was $7. Fruit sellers, cakes sellers, etc. were $5. Caterers, draymen, fishermen, porters, and day laborers' badges cost $4. Fisherwomen, washerwomen, and house servants badges were $2. There was a $20 fine to owners that did not purchase badges. As similar practice now exist with the peddlers licensing system and also gate passes having to be purchased for employees of Gullah/Geechee descent that go into the gated areas that are still called "plantations." Without these passes, they are not allowed entry in order to work even to clean houses, cut grass, cook, etc.

In life nor death could the people of African descent find a place of rest if they did not create one for themselves. This started a series of discussions of who was responsible for various things and what would be allowable in Charleston. "The responsibility for providing a suitable burial place for Negroes was considered to be the duty of the public authorities rather than the church. When it was brought to the attention of the intendants that the graveyard set aside for Negroes was filled, the Board [of Police] recommended that its secretary write to the commissioners of streets 'requiring them to look out for and set apart some proper place as a burying ground for Negroes." (McCowen p.40) They wanted to keep Charleston's appearance clear of the view of the negro when travelers came through:

"But British travelers were most interested in Charleston's Negro residents. Visitors were struck immediately by the great number of Negroes they saw in the streets. Indeed, it seemed to some observers that the blacks out-numbered the whites in the city. George Ranken, for example, reported that the 'great number of darkies is very striking at first. You see, even in the main streets, two or even three of these to every white man, and in the back streets you see no one else. Charleston, like other southern cities, did not permit Negroes to be in the streets after nine o'clock in the evening. At that time, the ringing of the bells of St. Michael's Church and the beating of drums at the headquarters of the city guard notified all Negroes without passes to return to their homes. Those who remained in the streets could anticipate being locked up for the night and flogged by the city guard. In addition to the restriction upon the black population, J Benwell claimed in 1853, that they also were prohibited from walking on the sidewalks, and the men were required to 'salute every white they ever met.' He pointed out that although these regulations were 'falling into disuse,' they had not yet been abolished. Thus, he recalled having seen 'several negroes from the plantation districts, walking in the road instead of on the pavement, in accordance with this law, touching their hats to every white passer-by; they were consequently obliged to be continually lifting their hands to their heads, for they passed white people every step.' With regulations such as these, it was not surprising that Barnwell would observe that the 'general appearance of the majority of the coloured people in the streets of Charleston denoted abject fear and timidity...

Several English visitors attended slave auctions while in Charleston. It was noted that these sales took place outdoors in the vicinity of the Exchange. There was a 'large house' in this area, where the slaves were 'lodged and taken care of,' according to John Vesey. This was, he stated, a 'sort of depot for slaves where there are always some on sale, and where you can purchase one at any time, or at the auctions that take place weekly.' George Ranken, like others among his countrymen, visited slave auction out of curiosity, but then viewed the proceedings with abhorrence. 'The scene,' he wrote, 'was most painful, humiliating, and degrading. I became quite affected myself, and was obliged to hurry away, for fear of showing what I felt.'

A walk down to the docks brought the English visitor into contact with the basis of the Charleston economy. The city functioned as a major port for the exportation of cotton and rice. This was facilitated by Charleston's excellent harbor, which, George Ranken noted, was 'well sheltered by islands, and a projecting tongue of land.

***The port, he observed, was crowded with ships, 'principally from Liverpool and Greenock,' which were being loaded with 'huge and multitudinous bales [of cotton] for the mills of Manchester and Glasgow...' These vessels he claimed, brought coal from England and Scotland in exchange for cotton." (The South Carolina Historical Magazine 1970 Vol. 71 No. 1 Charleston, SC "Charleston in the 1850s: As Described by British Travelers" by Ivan D Steen p.44-45)

Much of this cargo got aboard these vessels by being placed there by the enslaved. The enslaved worked on and operated everything from the boats to wagons to the railways. "Southern railroad companies headquartered in cities held large numbers of bondsmen for railway repair and construction work. The South Carolina Railway in Charleston owned 103 slaves in 1860." (Before Freedom Came 127)

In Charleston between 1850 and 1870, 27% of the adult male population were skilled artisans. In carpentry and masonry, the people of African descent outnumbered the Anglos. Many were involved in architecture and engineering. In 1848 all 706 enslaved artisans were male. Many of these artisans were able to keep some funds from the money that came in from their work. They then used this to have some semblance of freedom in the city once they completed their daily tasks.

By 1850, the planter class felt that Gullah/Geechees of the City of Charleston were out of hand. They wanted "owners" to move them onto the islands. They tried to restrict their movements and activities in order to control them as well. They felt that the city bred discontent and independence which were ingredients of insurrection. They had yet to see what happened when these ingredients were finally heated up by the fire that would shoot from the guns finally signaling the day of Jubilee and actually giving them just what they asked for-a return of these Africans to the islands.

Roung de Sitee:
 The Islands and Townships of
  Charleston County, South Carolina

Charleston County, South Carolina consist of both mainland and a special series of barrier islands that are called the "Sea Islands." The area is a portion of what is also referred to as the "Lowcountry." Charleston, South Carolina's islands were the place of both the death of indigenous or Native American culture along its coastline and the birth of the Gullah/Geechee culture from and on its soil. The Gullah/Geechee Nation came together through the vision of many that dwell on these islands and was solidified on Sullivan's Island.

Sullivan's Island sits "just down the way" from an area that was first called, "Onisecaw." This was the name that the island that is now called "Bull Island" bore before the coming of Stephen Bull from Britain in March of 1670. The island and the bay that brought the British into the area got renamed in honor of Bull to "Bull's Bay" and "Bull's Island."

What is now called "Bull's Island" was a hunting ground by the Sewee Native Americans. There are no records of treatise wherein the Sewee relinquished their claim to this land area. However, in 1696 Bull's Island was part of two warrants that were issued by the British:

By the Govern You are forthwith to measure or cause to bee admeasured & Laid out unto Collo Thomas cary a Plantacon Containineing Eight hundred acres of Land or thereabouts which plantacon is situate upon the Sea Cost to the Northward of Ashley river & is an island commonly called Bullings Island for which the sd Collo: Thomas Cary hat already paid the Lords Pprs: Sixteene pounds Currant Money & if the sd: Island Shall containe More than Eight hundred acres aforesd: then the sd Cary is to pay so much more in Pporcon after that rate if Less so much Porconally to bee returned & You are to observe the Lords Pprs: instruccons to the Survr & a Platt & Certificate of the sd island you are to returne into the Secrty's office that a grant may bee made for the Same & for Yor So Doing this Shall be yor Warr: Given undr my hand & Seale att Charles Towne the 2d day of October 1696 John Archdale Survr Genll: or his Depty." [sic]

Mr. Samll: Hartly had a Warrt: out of

the Secrtys office for an Island commonly called anisecau or Bullings Island which wart: is Dated the 7th of December 1696." [sic]

A deed dated July 4, 1698 was conveyed to Thomas Cary by Samuel Hartley that gave "all that ye sd. Island commonly called oni-se-cau containing One Thousand Five hundred & Eighty Acres of Land." On November 14, 1706, Thomas Cary for and in Consideration of the full & Just Sum of one hundred & thirty pounds Currt Money of the said province aforesd: vintner'...'all that the island aforesaid Containing One Thousand five hundred & Eighty Acres of Land.' John Collins was the Provost Marshal of South Carolina at a point.

Bull's Island was utilized as a lookout point from at least 1707 to 1711. Sewee and other indigenous Americans kept watch along with one white man. The tabby remains on the island are believed to be from the fortification that was placed there in the midst of the plantation that also contained livestock. John Laurens had written a letter to his uncle, James Laurens to let him know that his father had written to tell him:

"The Active was the last of the Enemy's

Fleet on the Coast-she went with a Tender to Bull's Island landed 40 white and 20 black men, kill'd by platoon firing a few head of Cattle, augmented their black Guards by stealing six Negroes; and went off."

During the American Revolution, Thomas Shubrick of Charles Town, who was a member of the Commons House of Assembly of the Provincial Congress of the state, purchased the island from Collins for four thousand two hundred and fifty pounds on April 26, 1792. He wanted to have all of the livestock driven off the island once he took ownership of it. In his will, he left the island to his second son, Thomas to be sold. Interestingly enough, during the war, Thomas had been commanded by Colonel Francis Marion for whom the "Francis Marion National Forest" is named. This forest and the *Cape Romain National Wildlife Refuge* take up the majority of the Awendaw and Sewee areas today.

After numerous title transfers over the years, a section of the island came to be owned by *Bannockburn Plantations Corporation*. This corporation was owned by Mr. Gayer G. Dominick of New York City. He had the "Dominick House" built there during 1926-1927. It later became a hunting lodge which essentially brought it back to the use that the Sewee had for it originally. The house was opened on a concession basis at one point in the history of the Cape Romain NWR. However, policy changes and budgeting caused it to be closed in 1969.

Some of the Gullah/Geechees of Awendaw worked on the island before it became the NWR. Mr. Jack Simmons would let people know of some of the history of the island which also included a "hanging tree." The energy of this tree and the history of the plantation there was no doubt a part of why the people left there to head for the mainland once the Civil War began.

"Moore's Landing" is the point from which boats now leave to go over to Bull's Island. However, many of those in Awendaw that live closer to Highway 17 can recall when that area was an all Gullah/Geechee area and their family members raised their families there. Many moved closer to the main road over time in order to have more access to people passing by that would buy goods, seafood, and vegetables from them. The land near the water was poorer soil and prone to flooding. So, they went to "higher ground" literally and figuratively.

Awendaw which became an incorporated town on August 18, 1992 has also had its name written as "Owendaw" in the past. The center has even been written of as "Avendaughbough," "Awendaughbough," and "Auendau." The name of the area is a name that means "deer" or "gun meat" that came from the language of the indigenous Americans called the "Sewee." The Samp, Santee, Sewee, and Wando were in this area long before the Anglos came. Sewee language is a form of Siouan which was the group that the Sewee descended from. The shell rings of this rich people still remain as the evidence of their existence along the coastline of what is now often called "Sewee to Santee."

Awendaw Barony was also known as "Salt Hope Plantation" and "Salt Pond Plantation," named for the 'salt ponds' at Bull's Bay (also called "Sheeawee" or "Sheeaway") on Awendaw Creek. They were 1,040 and 1,100 acre tracts respectively. When the 12,000 acres were granted to Sir Nathaniel Johnson in 1709 it was called "Sewee Barony." He tried to make salt by evaporation at one of the plantation there. He later sold the area to Peter Manigault who lived at "Manigault Barony" until he died in the Civil War.

The area came to be known by the names of different plantations that it consisted of. Murphy's Island was a cotton and rice plantation unto itself. The coastal area came to be split into such names as "Walnut Grove," "Kensington," "Buck Hall," "Laurel Hill," Doe Hall," "Kit Hall," "The Point," Oak Grove,"

"Palmetto," "Ormond Hall," "Bellfield," Blue House," "Wambaw," Springfield," Washoe and Cape," Eldorado," Indianfield," "Harrietta," Egremont," "Woodville," "The Wedge," "Palo Alto," "Bellevue," "Fairfield," Peachtree," "Peafield," "Montgomery," "Romney," "Hampton," "Elmwood," "Waterhorn," Millbrook," "Cedar Hill," "Woodstock," Islington," "Woodville," "Lynch's Ferry," and "Tibwin."

Tibwin Plantation on Tibwin Creek (a branch of the Harbor River) in Awendaw is off US 17 in the *Francis Marion National Forest* as well. It began in 1705 as a 2,500 acre plantation. Cotton and rice were both harvested at this location by the many families that still live near the house that is on the remaining property. It was built in 1805. When the 1,082 acre adjoining Doe

Plantation was added to this estate, another house was built there. When the property was sold to *Palmetto Land Development Corporation*, it was split into Tibwin and South Tibwin.

Henry Ford purchased the water powered rice mill from Tibwin between 1940 and 1942. It is now on display in Dearborn, Michigan. In 1995 the *United States Forestry Service* acquired the now 512 acre Tibwin. This place was recommended as a location for an interpretive center for Gullah/Geechee culture by the *National Park Service* in spite of the Gullah/Geechee peoples firm and consistent objections to this or any other sites that were recommended being utilized. This showed the Gullah/Geechee people a clear mission of the agents of the *National Parks Service* that had been involved with the *Special Resource Study of Lowcountry Gullah Culture* to "museumize" and further commodify their culture.

"Two Cedar Plantation" on the Cooper River in Awendaw was the site of a motel which has been torn down; land is currently vacant. Prior to that, rice and cotton were harvested there.

Just as with the formation of South Santee, Germantown, Beehive,

Gadsonville, and Hamlin Beach, the Gullah/Geechees that had been enslaved there did not move too far when settling onto land of their own, the Gullah/Geechees that descended from the plantation that was formed at Bull's Island by John Collins are those that migrated to the areas now called "Awendaw" and "McClellanville." Many of the historic homes there were built by Julian Brown who was a Gullah/Geechee architect that did a great deal of building in his area during the early twentieth century.

In 1685 or thereabout, French Huguenots came to occupy what is not the McClellanville area. King Jeremy of the Sewees was still in the area at that time, but with the influx of the Anglo people, the Sewee population began to diminish. By 1730 a Colonial Lynch was came to settle their area and set off into rice production. By 1762 a rice plantation was fully established there.

In the 1750s, Lynch and his family moved their "summer home" to the Cape Islands. Archibald McClellan and his wife purchased the land that they had from them. McClellan started to lease out parcels of land to planters of the South Santee region which lead to the formation of "McClellanville."

McClellanville began as the R.T. Morrison's Jeremy Tract (1858) and the A. J. McClellan's Tract. It was further divided into several plantations including "Peachtree Plantation" on the South Santee River. The two men sold waterfront lots. The Village was re-established as a fishing village, planter's retreat, and commercial center after the Civil War.

Wedge Plantation north of it is in both Charleston and George- town Counties and is named for its shape. The plantation house is located off US 17 on Wedge Plantation Road in the *Francis Marion National Forest*. The original rice fields are located across the South Santee River in Georgetown County. Clayfield Plantation is also in the *Francis Marion National Forest* as is "Fairlawn Plantation." This plot at the head of Wando River is a doughnut hole of privately owned land in the southern part of the forest. *Congaree-Carton Limited Partnership* has granted *The Nature Conservancy* a conservation easement on a 456-acre portion of Fairfield Plantation in *Charleston County Nature Conservancy*. Mary Alice Monroe's novel, *"Skyward,"* gives a fictional depiction of this area that was a 465 acre section at one point.

Amongst those that were part of the rice planters of the Saint James, Santee area in which McClellanville lies were the Pinckneys, Doars, Schoolbreds, Corders, Lucases, Gadsdens, Nowells, Rutledges, Manigaults, and Mazycks. (The latter two included Gabriel Manigault and Alexander Mazyck who refused to be a part of Reconstruction. They decided to move to Canada instead of adhering to the government laws that were being implemented. They died in Canada.) The Anglo men that owned these properties and the enslaved people as chattel often had their own social clubs. Opposite "Bellevue Plantation" in McClellanville and right on the river stood the clubhouse for an organization of these rice planters. This tradition of exclusive clubhouses on waterways still manifest itself as a part of the planning designs for each and every gated area of the Gullah/Geechee Nation.

These gated areas have become zones of escape for many of the people that live there and for those that rent the villas and/or resort and hotel rooms throughout the year. Although many see this as a fairly recent phenomenon, it has been in existence from the plantation era onward. These places to which Anglo people often go "on holiday" are around the world. During the plantation era a number of these places to which those of the "planter class" went from Charleston in order to be in cooler climates where a part of the "Pineland Villages." These included Edingsville (on Edisto Beach), Rockville, Adams Run (on South Edisto River), Centerville, Johnsonville, Legareville, Seccessionville (on James Island), Summerville, Cainhoy, Moultrieville, Mount Pleasant, McClellanville, Honey Hill, Cordesville, Spring Hill, Gravel Hill, Pineville, Pinopolis, The Barrows, Whitesville, and New Hope. These were places of refuge and social gatherings where numerous clubs were formed and gatherings were held.

In 1884 a group was formed called the *Agricultural Society of St. James Santee.* It replaced the *Planters Club.* These societies kept up with the others in their area that were a part of their economic class. For those that were not planters of rice and indigo, they came in and made their money from opening stores. "Silver Hill Plantation" was the home of John Boswell Skipper who came from Wilmington, North Carolina in 1858 and opened the first naval store in

McClellanville.

The saw mills became mechanisms of industry in the McClellanville area. These started to be erected there as early as the Revolutionary War. Millbrook on Wambaw Creek and also Marsh Island contained one.

"Hampton Plantation" on Wambaw Creek (a branch of the South Santee River) on Rutledge Road is a South Carolina State Historic Site due to the fact that it dates back to 1735. This was the home of Harriott P. Horry who was the daughter of Charles and Eliza Lucas Pinckney. She owned Harrietta Plantation between Collins Creek and the South Santee River which became a plantation in 1735. She had a home built there in 1797 for her daughter, Harriott H. Rutledge. The main crop was rice.

"Laurel Hill Plantation" had the same focus as these 3500 acres were cleared along the Harbor River at 8913 Highway 17 North. It became a bed and breakfast inn in 1986. Fairfield Plantation in the opposite direction on Highway 17 was 993.5 acres where Thomas Lynch built his home in 1730.

"Doe Hall Plantation," which began in 1851 as a rice plantation, is the home of the house from Laurel Hill Plantation. It was moved there in 1982. Two conservation easements, totaling 225 acres, on portions of Doe Hall Plantation near McClellanville have created a habitat corridor along U.S. Highway 17 between the *Francis Marion National Forest* and the *Cape Romain National Wildlife Refuge*. The properties, owned by Harrington W. Morrison and Ellias Horry Morrison and Dorothy D. Morrison, provide habitat for neotropical migratory birds and migratory waterfowl and are hydrologically linked with the Bulls Bay estuary which is designated a Western Hemisphere Shorebird Reserve.

McClellanville and Awendaw are both small townships with large Gullah/Geechee populations that tend to live quiet lifestyles keeping themselves sustained from the waterways and the land. With the incorporation of the towns, there have also come struggles for control of the future uses of the land. Corporations have already set their eyes on the land in the area and intend to build gated areas and subdivisions that could then end the seafood industry and displace many of the families. If this happens, the few stories that still remain tucked away in the small *Village Museum* may be the only ones to locate because the living books will have to move to other points north, south, and west.

The Gullah/Geechees of Mount Pleasant have greatly been impacted by the displacement that has been caused by the influx of subdivisions and tourists. The heart of the Town of Mount Pleasant is called the "Village." Mount Pleasant was settled in 1680. In 1798 James Hibben purchased Mount Pleasant Plantation, near the ferry and had it surveyed and divided into 35 tracts. Lucasville, Greenwich, Hilliardsville, Hibben's Ferry Tract, and Mount Pleasant merged into today's Mount Pleasant.

"Mount Pleasant Plantation" began in 1803 as a division of the Jacob Motte estate. Before this Mt. Pleasant included plantations such as Long Point Plantation which was a 1719 cotton plantation. There also was "Starvegut Hall Plantation" on the Wando River is within the northwestern portion of Dunes West development in Mount Pleasant. In 1759 this was a 1,080 acre rice plantation run by 50 enslaved Africans.

"Belleview Plantation" that began in 1735 and once was the enslavement zone of 38 Africans was once called "New Bermuda." The land was purchased prior to 1979 from *Georgia Pacific* and developed in 1979 as the Wando Port.

"Boone Hall Plantation" on Boone Hall Creek on Long Point Road began in 1681 when Major John Boone was given a land grant. The house that thousands of tourist visit now is not the 1790 wooden house that was existed. Horlbeck Brickyard where John and Henry had enslaved Africans working, supplied the bricks of the current buildings that are throughout what was once a 4,000 acre cotton plantation.

Across from Boone Hall is "Snee Farm." Although it is now a subdivision, most people that live there or pass by do not realize that it was a 800 acre plantation. Amongst the approximately fifty enslaved Africans at this location, most were documented according to their skills. The plantation was operated by a driver, sawyer, carpenter, field worker, cooper, and gardener. They lived in cabins at the site which no longer stand. A part of it is now the *Charles Pinckney National Historic Site*. Pinckney's house was built there in 1754.

"Hamlin Plantation" was once also called "Youghal" just as "Oakland Plantation" on Copahee Sound was. The latter got its name from John Perrie, an Irishman, named his plantation Youghal or Younghall for his birthplace in Cork County, Ireland. The name was changed to Oakland about 1850 because of the majestic "cathedral" type of oak avenue leading to the house. Now a Super *Walmart* is to occupy this location along with the plantation house in which a family still dwells. The plantation was started in, but the house was built in 1740. It is believed to the oldest house in the Christ Church Parish.

In 2004 the Gregorie Family and *Avtex Commercial Properties, Inc.* broke ground on "The Avenues at Oakland Plantation." The design focuses on preserving open space with a conservation easement, preserving the historical home and grounds, offering greater traffic connectivity, new retail services and further economic development for the community. Seventy-five acres are intended for commercial office and retail development and 236 acres of the original 982 acres have been set aside for conservation easement and will be placed with the Mt. Pleasant Open Space Foundation.

This 876 acre area is one of the major homes of the traditional sweetgrass basket makers.

The heart of culture in the town has been kept alive in sections called "Hamlin," "Six Mile," "Seven Mile," "Eight Mile," and "Ten Mile." "Phillips," "Greenhill," "Snowden," and "Scanlonville" along with these areas are all seeking to hold their ground, their seawork, and their sweetgrass traditions as the cost of taxes continues to increase all around them.

Commercial zoning along Highway 17 has already cut into the economic system that these communities have had since Reconstruction. Many of the sweetgrass basket making families have or had stands along this main road until the highway needed to be expanded to accommodate for increased traffic. They also had to move entirely from a strip that would become a major shopping "city" not just a mall.

In order to try to keep their tradition and economic livelihood going, collectives of sweetgrass basketmakers have been formed. Amongst the roll call of these families keeping this aspect of the Gullah/Geechee culture alive, you will read names such as Coakley,

Lee, Smalls, Wright, Scott, Richardson, Habersham, and Manigault and many more. Joyce V. Coakley who is an educator from Mount Pleasant, took the time to document the oral histories of this area. As a result of a number of years of work, she has come forth with a book entitled, "Sweetgrass Baskets and the Gullah Tradition." This is the first work that has been done on this tradition from the perspective of an actually Gullah/Geechee. It depicts the imagery illustrated with the words of the people.

Many of the people of Mount Pleasant have had their story told and their traditions exploited by non-Gullah/Geechees. Many of them can easily trace back those that first brought forth the tradition of exploitation by simply tracing back their last names. One such example is with the name "Manigault." An Anglo man named, Gabriel Manigault was a major merchant. He owned and "handled" some slaves, but preferred to stick to the importation of rum, sugar, wines, oils, fabrics, and flour. He exported rice, pitch, tar, turpentine, lumber, shingles, sole leather, deer skins, corn, peas, beef, and pork. He had shops on Tradd Street. He was the son of Pierre Manigault who also was a trader. Charles Izard Manigault, James Reid Pringle, John Berkeley Grimball, and many others were "slave traders" and plantation owners whose names can still be found listed in telephone directories of Mount Pleasant and various other areas of Charleston County, South Carolina.

Like Manigault, the Gullah/Geechees of Mount Pleasant were and continue to be enterprising people. This spirit lived in:

• Tweedy who was a seafood street vendor and Solomon Smith also sold seafood.

• Henry McNeill who was the driver of the stage coach, The Ominbus. He also was a news carrier for the News and Courier. He had the first telephone in Mt. Pleasant.

• Amanda Switzer, Mary Robinson, Lizzie Jenkins, Sarah Ann Thompson, and Rozella Wilson were all midwives.

• Edmund Jenkins was the town marshal. Sam Stinney was his assistant and was also a bus driver. James Hopkins succeeded Jenkins.

• Adam Bennett was the sexton for the St. Andrews Episcopal Church and he also played the organ. The Baptist Church burned down in 1877 along with the house of the sexton, George Jefferson Carter.

• Peter Simmons was the blacksmith for the village.

• James Hopkins was the lamplighter for the village. When he lit the lights, the children knew that it was time to go home.

• Lubkin was the shoemaker.

• Tony Aiken and Guy Timms sold vegetables.

• Scotland Smalls was a handyman.

• Maggie Mazyck of the Liberty Hill section was a flower vendor.

• Paul Jerman was a chimney sweep. The person doing this job was also called a "Ro Ro."

• Anthony B. Summersill was the postmaster in 1884.

• Charles Lafayette was the court crier who blew a horn from the ironwork balcony of the Court House for the opening of each day's session.

- Isaac Harris was the jailer.

"Boone Hall" and "Snee Farm" were major plantations from which many of the Gullah/Geechees of Mount Pleasant descended from. Both of these plantations are now major historic sites. Boone Hall is considered the "most filmed plantation in America."

Snee Farm which was a rice plantation that was owned by Charles Pinckney has now been divided between a subdivision and a national historic site. The Pinckney name has been placed on castles (as in the case of the one on Folly Island that dates back to 1799), streets, and many other areas throughout the Gullah/Geechee Nation due to the fact that this was one of the major slaveholding families in the region. This is also one of the reasons that you find Gullah/Geechees as well as Anglo-Carolinians that bear that last name.

Entire townships also bear the names that Gullah/Geechees took on after having been stripped of their original African names or having lived lives without surnames. "Scanlonville" takes its name from John Scanlon. Scanlon was a freedman that purchased 614 acres of what had been "Remley Plantation" in the area of Mount Pleasant. He bought the land at an auction in 1868 for $6100.

Scanlon founded the *Charleston Land Company* to provide land ownership for other freedmen. He then started the traditions of subdivisions in the area when he divided up the area into lots for the community to be laid out according to a plan just as many of the ones that are now displacing people are laid out. "Planned Unit Developments" or PUDs are a major term used in building and zoning departments throughout the Gullah/Geechee Nation. However, these are not for Gullah/Geechees generally, but for those that are coming from other areas to live in the region. During the 1870s, Scanlon's planned community included number streets and avenues as well as a graveyard, a farming area, a park and a wharf called "Remley's Point." The graveyard has been under attack due to incoming PUDs. The "destructioneers" also known as "developers" have been in a court battle with the community because they want to move the graves in order to build houses where the hallowed ground is. This burial area has been proven to be a historic site by the *National Register of Historic Places*. However, that designation would no longer stand if the graves are moved nor does a designation prevent the destruction of historic areas.

Scanlonville has been noted as a historic area by the *South Carolina Department of Historic Preservation*. However, "Green Hill Community," Snowden, and Phillips have had to place their own signs to acknowledge their historic existence while they continue to seek to have the state acknowledge them as well. These towns sit amidst modernity that makes it easy for people to pass by and through and not realize the history that they have held on to.

Phillips was established in 1878. It took its name from the plantation that the ten acre parcel that became the small village came from. A group of freedmen bought this part of Phillips Plantation for $63.00. Phillips Plantation had been a part of Laurel Hill and Boone Hall Plantations. John Rutledge who came from Ulster, Ireland married into the Boone Family by taking Sarah Boone Hext as his wife. He then received land as was often a part of dowries and such during those times. The Rutledge name is not uncommon amongst Sea Islanders. It is a common surname and a name on streets and such. This name is also on the *United States*

Constitution and the *Declaration of Independence* since Sarah and John's sons, John and Edward, respectively, signed these documents. They bother served in the first and second Continental Congresses and were governors of the State of South Carolina. The tomb of John Rutledge is located in Phillips Community.

Their descendants still remain on the land to this day, as is the case with most of the family compounds that exist throughout the Gullah/Geechee Nation. Most families hold 10, 20, 40, or 100 acre plots in common. This structure has brought forth a major legal dilemma in dealing with issues of "heir's property."

Another issue that comes into play for Gullah/Geechees is maintaining control over their burial areas as outside individuals come into the region. Phillips is no different. Their traditional burial area is located on Parker Island. The *"River Town Country Club"* has desecrated their burial areas there and have gated out the descendants.

Although cemetery desecration is a felony offense, many counties will not prosecute unless one individual is caught "red handed." There have been rare occasions where the community members have pressed the issue long enough in court and won suits against individuals and companies that have caused these violations. The Gullah/Geechees of Phillips would have to go by boat to lie in wait to see what is happening give then fact that those that built the country club had their bridge that went to Parker Island destroyed when the country club was built. The entire community will be destroyed if the people there do not truly link with their own nation. The *Town of Mount Pleasant* sees a need to change SC Highway 41 to deal with the traffic problems that they are facing and this would cause major impact on what remains of the Phillips Community.

These traffic problems will persist as tourists continue to come to the area. Unfortunately, many of them do not come for the true value of the community-the lives of the Gullah/Geechee people. A lot of them simply track down some sweetgrass baskets from Market Street in historic downtown Charleston or as they head northward to shop in Mount Pleasant without truly asking these families that make the baskets how they have kept these traditions alive and kept their families in tact in the area. The visitors are usually more interested in picking up a trinket and proceeding out to the beaches such as those at Folly Beach or to the gated areas of Seabrook and Kiawah. Daniel Island which is the birthplace of Smithsonian fellow and Gullah/Geechee blacksmith, Phillip Simmons and colonial Baptist minister, Richard Furman is on its way to catching up to these recreational areas as well. Even the obscure islands such as "Drum Island" that is near Daniel Island are being sought after in order to accommodate the coming floodtide. However, this floodtide is not that of water. It is that of people.

In the past, those that were in Charleston would run to Summerville in the summer months, but they are now finding that there is no place to run. The islands such as James Island, the towns of Hollywood and Ravenel, and beyond are experience the influx of those that can no longer afford to live on the peninsula or even surrounding islands such as John's and Wadamalaw as the families are displaced or lose their land for non-payment of taxes.

Many of the islands have formed their own community action groups and associations. These associations consistently find themselves having to educate and re-educate the people of their areas concerning the zoning issues that are happening around them and how this will affect them. Edisto Island has to deal with this issue in more than one county since its main area sits in the boundaries of Charleston County, but its beaches are not. These beaches which include "Botany Bay" have not only been captured in films such as Columbia Picture's, *"The Patriot"* with Mel Gibson, but have been caught in zoning battles also.

Edisto Island was home to the "Edistows" which were the indigenous people of the area. They got displaced as the British came in and started to gain charters to the areas. In 1714 the Carolina legislature voted approval for "a highroad and causeway to be built from John Frip's [sic] Edisto plantation to Wilton." This was an indigo plantation because the attempts at growing rice there continually failed.

Many of those that gained their wealth in indigo lost it when the American Revolution began against England. England had been the primary market for this product. They paid bonuses to planters for it. These bonuses helped the Grimballs, Seabrooks, Jenkins, Frampton's Mikells, Wilkinsons, Whaleys, Baynards, Baileys, and many others to rise into the planter aristocracy.

William Aiken who was the elected governor of South Carolina in 1844, was one of the largest enslavers of Africans in the south. He operated a rice plantation at Jehossee which was once a part of Little Edisto Island until it became severed by the Dawhoo Cut. Not far from here was also a sea island cotton plantation on Raccoon Island. This island was later converted to a lodge.

Aiken and others that "owned" the major plantations of Edisto Island did not want to see the Gullah/Geechees obtaining them. Even when offers were made by the freedmen to purchase the land, they were refused. One man sold his portion of the island to them and moved away. This allowed "Freedmen's Village" to be established not far from Edisto Beach.

The beaches of Edisto are also in the many memories of celebrations of Gullah/Geechees that would go on bus rides to these places and enjoy themselves in celebration together. The parties also took place at Riverside in Mount Pleasant near Remley's Point and at Mosquito Beach on James Island.

The sounds of Sea Island soil gave birth not only to the spirituals that are now official "South Carolina's State Music," but also to many outstanding musicians. Many of the musicians that came from these islands were the ones that were hired for entertainment for the community gatherings, but those with the desire to have the world hear their sounds decided to cross the waters. One that crossed the waters from Edisto and headed north to Detroit, Michigan was James Jamerson.

The late Jameson became a legendary bassist who played on many Sixties hits from Motown Records as part of the label's classic rhythm section "The Funk Brothers". Jamerson is renowned for creating brilliant electric basslines that were breathtakingly complex and perfectly executed. As a result of his outstanding gift, he was the first bassist to be inducted into the *Rock and Roll Hall of Fame* in the "Sideman" category when it was created in 2000. James Jamerson was not there to accept his award because he had died of pneumonia in 1983. According to a *Detroit Free Press* article published shortly after his death, Jamerson had been shut out of studio work due to alcohol-related problems.

In spite of the problems, Jamerson left a history that has been examined in the book *"Standing in the Shadows of Motown."* It is a study of Jamerson's performances. However, the documentary bearing the same name is a mixture of interviews concerning all of the "Funk Brothers" with that of live performances by contemporary artists doing songs that the "Funk Brothers" sound made famous while they were not acknowledge as much as the singers that they backed up.

As a proliferation of the reconstructed plantations begin to dot the coastline in the townships and on these islands of Charleston, the sounds of Gullah/Geechees are becoming less and less audible. Some of what people are seeing and hearing that is being labeled "Gullah" are imitations and impersonations that the community does not find "flattering." The true story of the precedents that many of these island people set, how they weathered the storms and held on to their families, histories, heritage and culture in these places is being hidden beneath the concrete that is being poured and the golf courses that are being laid. Even concrete can crack and when it does, that which has been growing beneath it has a chance to spring forth. The energy of the ancestors from these islands that stood up has started to spring forth so that the world will know that they realized that they had a right to hold on to their legacy which is the land!

Jublee dun cum!!!-Season of Celebration

Charlestown post office started in 1740. It must have seen a number of letters go out after "Big Shoot" began. This was the beginning of the Civil War that was going to bring a major change to the Sea Islands region once again. This was to be written about in letters, journals, and newspapers. Yet, the writers did not truly realize how these papers were not going to mean as much as the deeds that were about to be transferred would.

In December of 1860, Colonel Robert Anderson had a garrison from Fort Moultrie secretly occupy Fort Sumter. On January 9th a supply ship was bringing relief to Fort Sumter and was fired on. The Secession Convention meet at the Baptist Church in Columbia, South Carolina on December 19, 1860. However, an outbreak of smallpox caused them to move the meeting the next day to the Hall of St. Andrew's Society in Charleston. They then passed the Ordinance of Secession and signed it in the South Carolina Institute Hall on Meeting Street. Then on April 14, 1861 the fort was bombarded until it surrendered. All of this sounded the beginning of the war between the agricultural south and the industrial north.

General Robert E. Lee who was the commander of the Southeastern Department surveyed the area during late 1861 and found that trying to defend the area from Charleston to Florida (which is the Gullah/Geechee Nation) was impossible. A massive exodus of Anglos began instead of attempting a defense. They were given a timeframe for evacuation before the federal gunboats began patrolling at the end of the year because thereafter the guns would fire on all boats that were approaching.

Because of the changes in the dynamics that came because of the Civil War, the composition of documents would begin to reflect listings of people instead of "chattel." People of African descent would go from being listed as items to be disbursed as a part of people's wills to being listed as people who are property owners themselves. A glimpse at what early census records showed are a good indicator of how the initial "face" of Charleston was seen:

Charleston

1850

Mulattoes

Ann Mitchell
Margaret Lee
William Mitchell
E W Garden
Henrietta Garden
Julia Garden
Hannah Garden
Margaret E.
Ann Bentham
Rebecca Thomas
Edward Dereef
Carolina
Thomas Brodie
Thomas Marshall
R Dereef
Gardener Dereef
RE Dereef
Isabella (2)
Joseph
Caroline
Harriet
Joseph Dereef
Mary
Elizabeth
Abigal
Justina
Charlotte
Richard
Amelia Cornwell
William C DeWees
Eliza
Elizabeth
Edward
Constania

Francis
Lucetta Bearfoot?
William W Seymour-Tavernkeeper
Mary Ann Seymour
William S Semour-hairdresser
Mary Ann
Sarah L
Eliza I
Charlotte
Samuel W

1860

Charleston Neck St. Philips Parish
    Weavers and Harrisons are Indians
Ward 5 of Charleston
    Conwell, Dewees, Dereef, Maxwell, and Miller are Indians
6th Ward
    Mitchell is Indian and Alexander is Mulatto
7th Ward
    Taylor and Washington are mulatto.
    Edwards is Indian

1870

Smith, Johnston, Izard, Bell, Miller, Jones, Furgeson, Dereef, Savage, and Mitchell are Indian and Smith is Black. Charles Millers wife and children are mulattoes as is Johnston

Ward 8
    Isaac Toomer's Family is black

1900 Ward 5 Ryan's are Indian with some blacks in the family

The ways in which to deal with the dynamics of race and ownership in Charleston were to erupt into a major issue that would last generations. The plantation era was beginning to come to an end. During the last six months of 1863 sales of Africans that had continued to be smuggled in to the Sea Island region fell off and there were those that had run from the area to points west and south that were waiting to hear that things had returned to normal and that business would go back to being the usual. However, that day would not come even after the smoke of Big Shoot had cleared.

On July 10, 1863 Union troops departed from Folly Island and landed on Morris Island to attach Battery Wagner. The 54th *Massachusetts Regiment* had already had a skirmish on James Island on July 16 where they lost 35 men. At dawn on July 18 the Union Army and Navy began a ten hour artillery bombardment. The 54th Mass spearheaded the attack. 1,500 Union casualties of which 272 (40%) were part of the 54th Massachusetts regiment.

The men that died at this battle as

well as their leader, Colonel Shaw were immortalized in the film *"Glory."* They are all buried in a common grave on Morris Island. Now people want to build a resort for recreation on top of these souls that should be honored. This would literally bury how many people of African descent were on the front lines.

In addition to those going to battle, 400 people of African descent worked at Morris Island in 1863 at once. Requisitions for "Negroes" were made to construct batteries and forts to the tune of 2500 per month. These funds went to those that had enslaved the Africans. Were it not for their skilled labor, Charleston could have easily been taken from the beginning.

As the battles continued, the people of African descent were pulled into the ranks more and more. The enslaved were to be "impressed" by the Confederate Congress after "free Negroes" had been. None of the enslaved were to be taken without the "owner's" permission. Full compensation was to be made for the enslaved that were lost through death or escape to the enemy while in government employ.

Amongst the rolls of people listed in

"Confederate Pensioners 1923-1925 by Alexia Jones Helsley" which was printed in 1998 by the South Carolina Department of Archives & History were:

Jim	Allston	Cain Hoy	Camp Attendant	
Paul	Campbell	James Island	Body Servant	James Island
Scipio	Casey	71 Kracke Street	Body Servant	Morris Street Baptist
Jim	Collins	Mt. Pleasant	Cook	
Cato L.	Drayton	91 St. Philip Street	Cook	
Isaac	Drayton	Charleston	Servant	
James	Giles	133 Wentworth Street	Cook	Morris Street Baptist
Jethro	Jenkins	Mt. Pleasant		
S.W.	Ladson	Adams Run	Cook	
Sam	Mack	279 Ashley	Cook	

		Avenue		
John	McKinley	Charleston	Private in Charleston Riflemen	
Louis	Middleton	18 Montague Street	Cook	
Wallace	Mikell	18 Pine Street	Camp Attendant	
Peter	Poinsette	26 Hamilton Street	Servant	
Daniel	Mack	Edisto		
John	Steed	Awendaw		

By 1865, 178,895 black soldiers had enlisted in the army. This was 12% of the North's fighting force. February 17, 1865 the Confederate Army finally abandoned Charleston after constant bombardment from the fort at Morris Island. The 54th Mass. mustered out of service on August 20, 1865 in Mount Pleasant.

In 1900 the United States government

issued the Medal of Honor to Sgt. William Carney making him the first black soldier to receive it. This was due to his service in the 54th Mass. Carney was 23 when he joined the army. He signed up because "I felt I could best serve my God by serving my country and my oppressed brothers."

The pride that Carney and the many others had in fighting on behalf of their kinspeople was evident in many ways. Those that had enslaved them previously did not take to this well at all. In fact, Henry W. Ravenel for whom the Ravenel area of Charleston, South Carolina is named, stated right after the Civil War:

"It is impossible to describe the condition of the city-It is so unlike anything we could imagine-Negroes shoving white persons off the walk-Negro women drest [sic] in the most outré style, all with veils and parasols for which they have an especial fancy-riding on horseback with negro soldiers and in carriages. The negro regiments have just been paid off which gives them money to indulge their elegant tastes..."

After having been refused the right to dress and adorn themselves in appropriate manner as their ancestors had been able to do at will in Africa, the people took full advantage of this.

However, the clothing was not the only example of this celebration of freedom.

"...early in the spring of 1865, when no one could doubt the outcome of the war any longer, Charleston's black community held a massive parade. Some four thousand took apart, including artisans, school-children, church and fraternal groups, firemen, and armed black soldiers. The procession stretched out for three miles, and one float in the parade told the essential story as it move along, bearing a coffin with a large sign, 'Slavery is Dead." Of course the parade said more. It was also another black announcement of the birth of freedom, stated not only in the signs, display, and songs, but in the major action itself: the gathering, marching, self-affirming movement of the former slaves. This was a sure indication that new times was coming. Black folks were moving literally and figuratively out of the side streets and the gutters, claiming the thoroughfares, claiming the right to parade, to beat their drums, to celebrate the reality of their freedom and resurrection, ultimately claiming the right to one another." (Harding p.274)

"The largest and most spectacular demonstrations took place in Charleston, less than a month after Union occupation. More than 4,000 black men and women wound their way through the city streets, cheered on by some 10,000 spectators, most of them also black. With obvious emotions, they responded to a mule-drawn cart in which two black women sat, while next to them stood a mock slave auctioneer shouting, 'How much am I offered?' Behind the cart marched sixty men tied together as a slave gang, followed in turn by a cart containing a black-draped coffin inscribed with the words 'Slavery is Dead.' Union soldiers, schoolchildren, firemen, and members of various religious societies participated in the march along with an impressive number of black laborers whose occupations pointed up the important role played in the local economy-carpenters, butchers, tailors, teamsters, masons, wheelwrights, barbers, coopers, bakers, blacksmiths, wood sawyers, and painters. For the black community of Charleston, the parade proved to be an impressive display of organization and self-pride. The white residents thought less of it. 'The innovation was by no means pleasant,' a reporter wrote of the few white onlookers, 'but they had sense enough to keep their thoughts to themselves." (Litwack p. 177)

A week after this celebration there was one for the ruins of Fort Sumter. January 1, 1866 more than 10,000 blacks assembled on a racecourse in Charleston to hear speeches and celebrate emancipation. They also continued in celebrating landownership as more than 40,000 of them settled in the area covered by Special Field Order No 15. (10,000 alone settled on Edisto Island.)

This field order covered "from Charleston and all the abandoned rice fields southward to Fernandina" [FL]. Amidst these miles of water and coastline were Wadmalaw, John's, James, and Edisto to name a few. Just as the Gullah/Geechees were settled into raising their families and their crops on their own, they were faced with yet another issue to challenge their new found free- dom.

On Edisto Island on Thursday, October 19, 1865 General Oliver O Howard of the *Freedmen's Bureau* attempted to carry out President Johnson's pardons of the slave owners. He had a meeting with some 1,000 people in the Episcopal Church on the island to announce this. The people sang, "*Nobody Knows the Trouble I Seen*" in response. Eventually he left and warned the whites that there would be bloodshed. Some still approached to meet with armed Gullah/Geechee people ready to fight to protect what they had given their blood, sweat, and tears for.

During Reconstruction, women of African descent in Charleston were "carrying axes or hatchets in their hands hanging down at their sides, their aprons or dresses half-concealing the weapons." A preacher warned that there are "80,000 black men in the state that can use Winchesters and 200,000 black women who can light a torch and use a knife."

"Abandoned by the once friendly government and faced with this brutal new policy, the people of the Sea Island region fought back as best they could. When four Northern speculators came to John's Island with a view of buying land from the old planters, they were surrounded by a constantly increasing crowd of angry Negroes. Men and women, with gun, pitchfork and club in hand, forced the visitors to march twelve miles across the island to the Bureau office where they were released.

When a party of white landlords came to Edisto Island to get the freedmen to contract to work their lands, they were received with threats of violence. The leader of the Negro farmers told the planters they would make no contract. The planters were warned not to remain on the island since a Negro who put them up for the night would surely have his house burned...When a group of planters visited James Island, in hope of convincing the freedmen to contract, they were met by forty armed Negroes, who drove them away. On a second visit they were accompanied by a captain of the *Freedmen's Bureau*. Again they were met with leveled guns and were held captive until the officer identified himself...When the planters came back a third time, the people used a new tactic. They saw that the mere presence of the planters on the island could effect nothing, so the two thousand islanders tried to stay out of sight...

'Wouldn't it be better for you to contract for good wages than work this way?' one person asked. 'No,' was the reply. 'I don't want to contract. I'll eat up my corn and peas first.' When it was pointed out that the farmer had only an old 'skin and bones' horse, the man answered, 'When he gets tired, I can plow the same as a horse.' An old couple working in a cotton field were asked what would they do if they could not get the land. The answer was the constant refrain of the Sea Island Negroes, 'If a man got to crost de riber and he can't git a boat, he take a log. If he can't own land, I'll hire or lease land, but I won't contract.' 'Come then,' said the planters to each other, 'we might as well go home." (Journal of Negro History Vol 41/1956 p.30-31)

The more that the freedmen were able to live and work amongst themselves, the more established they became. In most areas, the praise houses and the churches were the community centers. Reverend Richard H. Cain also wanted to establish a church in Charleston for freedmen. This became *Emmanuel Church*. This became a political organ in the state. Cain served in the state constitutional convention and the state senate. *Zion Church* was where the state wide black convention assembled in 1865.

The *Angelican Society for the Propogation of the Gospel* had begun their missionary work amongst enslaved Africans and indigenous Americans during 1701. In 1712 an Act made it lawful for the enslaved of South

Carolina to be baptized as Christians. Yet, the Anglos did all that they could to place restrictions upon the worship of the bondspeople and freedmen. There was legislation passed in the early 1800s to try to keep the African descendants in the churches that were lead and operated by the Anglos themselves.

In September 1865, a new African Methodist Episcopal Church cornerstone was laid by Robert Vesey, the son of Denmark Vesey. This was 40 years after their first church had been banished. 3000 clergy listened to speeches that day. By a year later, there were 11 "colored churches"-5 Methodist of which 2 were AME, 2 Presbyterian, 2 Episcopalian, 1 Congregational, and 1 Baptist. Some wealthy black families went to the *Methodist Episcopal Church* and some at *St. Mark's Episcopal*. *Morris Brown AME Church* was founded in 1867 by a small group of men and women that worshipped with the *Emmanuel AME Church* congregation. In 1873, under the leadership of Reverend Richard R. H. Cain, the church went to its present day location after they bought the plot. Ed Barber stated after the war:

"When I was trampin' 'round Charleston, dere was a church dere called St. Mark, *dat all de society folks of my color went to. No black nigger welcome dere, they told me. Thinkin' as how I was bright 'nough to git in, I up and goes dere one Sunday. Ah, how they did carry on, bow and scrape and ape de white folks...I was uncomfortable all de time though, 'cause they was too 'hifa-lootin' in de ways, in de singin', and all sorts of carryin' ons."*

Bethel African Methodist Episcopal Church was organized in 1867 in McClellanville by Reverend James Johnson along with Richard Harvey Cain, who was the presiding elder of the Charleston District. Daniel Payne was the bishop of the Bethel Howard Circuit. The original church was built in 1872. The architect and builder was the Gullah/Geechee architect of that area, Samuel Drayton. He also constructed the *Episcopal Chapel of Ease and* several homes in that area. This church was destroyed by a storm in 1917. Hurricane Hugo moved the next church from its foundation when it hit Charleston.

Mount Nebo African Methodist Episcopal Church of Awendaw was established on three acres of land in 1870 when Mr. Friday Reid and his sister Lucy Moultrie donated the land to the congregation. The current sanctuary opened in 1969 and the fellowship hall was added in 1977.

The *First Seewee Missionary Baptist Church* which was once known as "*Thy Kingdom Come*" started on Seewee Road in Awendaw in 1890. It had gained its independence from the *Morris Street Baptist Church* on December 12th of that year. This sanctuary was also damaged by Hugo, but still stands as a testimony to the original establishment.

Morris Street Baptist Church of Charleston had been the leading church of its denomination. It organized an association for churches and pray's houses in 1867. In 1876 there was a state- wide association which was spearheaded by the pastor of Morris Street, Jacob Legare and E. M. Brawley.

"John L. Dart was born a free Negro and graduated from *Avery Normal Institute* in Charleston as the valedictorian of its first graduation class in 1872. He then attended Atlanta University and the *Newton Theological Seminary* in Massachusetts. After teaching and preaching in the North and in Georgia, he returned to Charleston in 1886 to become the pastor of *Morris Street*

Church. In 1895 he founded the *Charleston Industrial Institute*, a school devoted to the vocational training of Negro youths. The building in which this school was conducted today houses the *Dart Hall Branch of the Charleston Free Library*." (Tindall, p. 205)

The churches and schools were not the only things established in Charleston, South Carolina. The *Freedmen's Bureau* also had headquarters there. The McLeod Plantation on James Island was a key location of one of these.

"In 1865 an officer of the *Freedmen's Bureau* stationed in South Carolina was confounded by the behavior of his black clients. He wrote to his superiors in Washington, DC, that former slaves from coastal plantations who had been relocated during the Civil War to inland sites 'were crazy to get back to their native flats of ague and country fever.

One South Carolina freedmen, after several years of service in the Union Army, did, in fact, return to take charge of a section of the plantation where he had previously lived and worked. Ignoring the protests of Thomas Pinckney, his former owner, he marched back to his old cabin and from its porch, rifle in hand, he declared, 'Yes, I gwi wuk right here. I'd like to see any man put me outer dis house.' Among emancipated slaves, freedom was presumed to go hand in hand with the right to own land, particularly the land they had worked for so many years. In a collective petition to President Andrew Johnson, a group of former slaves living in Edisto Island, South Carolina, clearly made this point when they protested the restoration of plantation lands to their former owners, declaring, 'This is our home. We have made these lands what they are.' Over and over again, newly emancipated blacks expressed a surprisingly intense connection to their former places of servitude." (Vlach, p. ix)

"Opposition to the Bureau first crystallized during the summer of 1865 as its officials undertook to re-settle hundreds of freedmen on lands that had formerly belonged to whites. Its control over such lands had grown out of wartime legislation by Congress, which had authorized Federal agents to seize certain kinds of property within the re-conquered areas of the Confederacy and then had directed that all such property be turned over to the

Bureau upon its creation. The Bureau was expected to distribute the land among freedmen by selling or leasing it to them in small plots and on convenient terms. Thereby a dual purpose might be served. Many of the former slaves would be encouraged to establish an economic independence with which to bolster their political freedom; and, secondly, the Bureau could use the income from such sales and rentals for the support of its work-a vital consideration, since Congress had not appropriated any money for its initial operations.

In South Carolina that total of such property at the disposal of the Bureau amounted to more than three hundred thousand acres of land. Under Saxton's direction agents and officers proceeded immediately to locate dozens of Negro families on forty-acre plots, either as tenants or as purchasers. The dispossessed white owners and their spokesmen promptly raised a sharp outcry against such proceedings. Typical was the comment of the Charleston Courier, which termed the presence of the Bureau 'anomalous and unnecessary' and then declared: 'Those are the real enemies of the Freedmen who seek to instill into them, that they can either be prosperous or progressive except by...frugality, sobriety, and honest, consistent toil.' Another paper echoed this view: 'We do not say that all Northern men who come South are of the class alluded to, but we do say that all who prowl through the country, teaching the Negroes...that the lands are to be given to the colored people...are the vilest and meanest sect that ever disgraced the annals of civilization.

In time the original owners were able to re-claim most of their property as a result of President Johnson's reconstruction policy, since the presidential program provided for a restoration of all rights, including those of property, to all who secured pardon." (The Proceedings of The South Carolina Historical Association 1962 Columbia, SC "The Freedmen's Bureau and Its Carolina Critics" by Martin Abbott p. 16)

"A planter made a typical plea calling for native whites to take 'the mental and moral development' of the freedmen into their own hands, so as 'to leave no room for the ingress of these Northern moths into the social hive'." (The Proceedings of The South Carolina Historical Association 1962 Columbia, SC "The Freedmen's Bureau and Its

Carolina Critics" by Martin Abbott p. 19)

In spite of these battles against re-enslavement, the freedmen continued to make progress. In 1886 1037 "Negro" depositors were a part of the bank. "In 1866, the Charleston branch of the Freedmen's Bank had deposits of $18,000; in 1870, $165,000, and in 1873, $350,000 belonging to 5,500 depositors, showing that this was the savings of the poor and not the capital of the petty bourgeois. Only about 200 of the depositors were white. The colored people had accounts ranging from 5 cents to $1000. When the bank failed in 1874, the Charleston branch owed 5,296 depositors a total of $253,168." ("Black Reconstruction in America 1860-1880" by W.E. B. DuBois 1962 Macmillan Publishing Company New York p. 416) Yet, in 1903, William Demosthenes Crum estimated that the "colored citizens" of Charleston owned in the aggregate over one million dollars worth of real and personal property and there was "hardly a street in the city that they do not possess and pay taxes on from one to thirty thousand dollars worth of real estate."

The funds had no doubt been accumulated through the income of the ship carpenters, coopers, barbers, candle and soap manufacturers, tailors, butchers, bakers, silversmithing, gun-smithing, harness-making, and chairmaking. In Charleston, people of African descent dominated the butcher's trade, barbering, shoemaking, and contracting until after World War I. In addition to these skills that were often done by men, people continued to farm. Women sold oysters, peaches, cakes, tarts, breads, milk, produce, fruit, sand, rice and other dry goods in the street.

"A. C. McClellan, like Crum, was reported in 1890 to have established an independent position in Charleston. He had graduated from *Howard Medical College* in the eighties, after having been a midshipman at Annapolis one year, and set up his practice in Charleston about 1884. In 1897 he founded the *Charleston Training School for Colored Nurses*, which still exists. The branch of obstetrical nursing in the school was under L. Hughes Brown, a graduate of the *Women's Medical College of Philadelphia*, and wife of a colored Presbyterian minister.

William Henry Johnson, born in Charleston in 1865, was awarded his M. D. by Howard University in 1887 and began practice immediately thereafter in Charleston. Joseph A. Robinson, a native of Charleston with free Negro background, graduated in 1893 from the *Medical School of Howard University* as an honor student, and returned to his native city to set up practice." (Tindall p. 148)

"Toward the end of the nineties several new experiments with Negro factory labor were made. An established knitting mill in Charleston, 'bowing before the imperative demand for cheap labor,' discharged its white employees in October, 1896, to hire Negro labor. By the following summer, there were eighty-five Negroes employed on sixty-five machines, turning out three hundred pairs of socks per day. The factory was reported to be running along smoothly and without the least trouble...In October, 1897 when wages for fifteen women in the *Charleston Shoe Factory* were changed from a weekly to a piecework basis, forty-five whites walked out, and Negro labor was called in to break the strike. The shoe factory was the third mill in Charleston to turn to Negro labor, for the *Charleston Cotton Mill*, after a protracted period of unprofitable operation, had begun to try Negro labor. The *News and Courier* saw in this as an important, maybe a dangerous experiment; but the reward would be so great should success follow that the hazard she [Charleston] takes is justified. Negro labor is the cheapest labor this country has ever known. Commercial progress and prosperity in these days demand cheap labor. Should Charleston discover that she can set a million spindles to humming in her midst by putting her colored population to work she will not only rid herself of an incubus, which has handicapped her hopelessly in the race for prosperity, but she will have blazed a way which her sister cities will not be slow to follow.

When intimated that they might resort to violence, the unsympathetic *News and Courier* reminded them that the mill community 'is too remote from other mills to hope for assistance. It is greatly outnumbered by negro laborers in Charleston, and in a 'race war' with the negroes would stand in need of protection. The operation of the *Charleston Cotton Mill*, however, continued to be unprofitable, and it was sold in 1899 to John H. Montgomery, a capitalist of Spartanburg.

Former white operatives issued 'threatening posters' and renamed *Vesta*

Cotton Mill, it was outfitted with new machinery and recommenced operations in 1899. The management appealed to colored ministers and other leaders of the Negro community to encourage Negro laborers to work in the mill, and it was operated through 1900 almost exclusively with Negro labor. The *Colored Ministers' Union* passed a resolution expressing appreciation of the opportunity presented, their race, and Negro leaders in Charleston, recognizing the significance of the experiment, did what they could to encourage Negroes to work efficiently in the mill. Girls employed were offered $7.80 a month while learning, after which they made from $12 to $15 per month. Tenements were offered at twenty-five cents per room per week...

George W. Williams, a prominent stockholder, noted... "The negroes, shunning 'the opportunity of their lives,' would go for oysters in the oyster season and then for strawberries in the strawberry season..." (Tindall p. 132-134)

What Williams did not realize was that the Gullah/Geechees did not see the opportunity to further enrich others as an opportunity of their lifetimes. The other seasonal businesses were true opportunities for them because they could get larger amounts of money in a faster period of time. They also could continue to have their time to themselves when they completed a job as they had become accustomed to. Many of them had their own land to tend to and homes to maintain on the islands and around the peninsula at this point.

When Reverend J. L. Dart of Charleston spoke at the founding meeting of the *"National Negro Business Men's League"* in 1900, he stated that there were approximately sixty "Negroes" engaged in business in his city. The capital of these was a quarter of a million dollars. There were 123 documented "Negro" businessmen at that time and half of them were in Charleston. This list included Charles C. Leslie who was a wholesale and retail dealer in fish, oysters, game, and poultry. He had two stalls in the fish market and offices at 18 and 20 Market Street.

For years, many traveled over from the islands on steamers to market goods and also to do days work as cooks, nurses, and housemaid and would return to their own homes and land. Numerous ferry companies operated over the years including William Seabrook's *Edisto Island Ferry Company* which in 1824 had its landing at Rockville at the end of Maybank Highway on Wadamalaw Island. *Mount Pleasant Ferry Company* went across the Cooper River.

In 1826 a ferry went from Little Edisto Island to the "Borough" area of Edisto Island. On February 22, 1907, the steamer, *Marion*, a coastwise ferry that went through the inland waterway on a regular schedule caught on fire. Many people from Edisto were on board and died in the fire including Reverend C. S. Caldwell. The burnt out hull of the ferry was rebuilt as *The Islander* after this tragedy occurred.

Many continued to gather at "Whooping Island" to catch ferries into the city until bridges were built so that people could drive across as more and more cars became available. Blacks generally worked at the docks and in cotton presses, drove vehicles, or worked as house servants. Farmers would take their goods over to trade throughout the peninsula with songs that often matched the produce or seafood that they had for sale.

Seafood was and is one of the many things that were shipped from the Charleston port. The port remains one of the main locations for larger grossing incomes amongst Gullah/Geechees in Charleston, SC until today. Gullah/Geechees have dominated the longshore industry there since prior to the Civil War. Due to the fact that Anglos have seen this work as inferior, they avoided it. Thus, in 1910 people of African descent had 92 percent of all longshoreman positions in South Carolina, Georgia, and Florida. Given that the Gullah/Geechees live along the waterways, they were the majority of this percentage and continue to be. Charleston ahs always had the largest numbers of people of African descent employed in this industry.

Although there are no records of a union of the longshoreman during 1865, ten years later they were noted as being "the most powerful organization of the colored laboring class in South Carolina" by a newspaper. The *Longshoremen's Protective Union Association* (LPUA) was formed in the middle of 1868. The South Carolina General Assembly issued it a legislative charter on March 19, 1869. It was rechartered in 1880. However, due to the political climate of Reconstruction, the charter was not renewed in 1900.

In June 1936, George Washington German led the effort to charter *International Longshoreman's Association Local 1422*. German had been the grandson of enslaved Africans. German focused on "Blacks" getting a higher education and then pursuing other endeavors. He did not want the focus to be placed on the union being mainly people of African descent.

German called upon Charleston Mayor William Morrison (1947-1959) to be the lawyer for the union. The interesting connection here is that Morrison's grandfather had owned German's grandfather and freed him in 1861. Morrison was the first to seek after the "Black" vote by appointing people of African descent to the police force and other city jobs. He extended sewer into the Gullah/Geechee areas of the city and built *Federal Housing Administration* properties in order to improve the way of life of many of the people in these areas. Working together through their long family connections, Morrison and German built a strong union.

The *ILA* continues to have a reputation of power. Kenneth Riley, a native Charlestonian Gullah/Geechee joined the local in 1977. Riley had already obtained a business degree from the *College of Charleston,* but went to work alongside his father. By 1980, he was the trustee of the local and by the early 1990s he was the vice president. Riley has served as the president of the local since 1997 after losing two previous elections for the seat. Riley keeps his focus on port issues and the rights of the people of his area and his union. He has been a driving force in keeping the Charleston port efficiently moving the commerce and trade from the "Holy City."

Trade was done at the docks and via boat to upcountry even during enslavement and this continued into Reconstruction. Because of the jealousy of this progress and their inability to put the people of African descent back in chains, Anglos petitioned to bring cases and set laws against merchants stating that some items were stolen and the like. As these petitions continued Black sociologist Ira De A. Reid, director of the National Urban League's Department of Research and Investigation, "discovered in Charleston, South Carolina, that black male laborers were 'losing constantly in all lines of work, particularly in building trades.' According to Reid:

Union men, particularly carpenters, have been known to walk off jobs when Negroes come on. White men are driving wagons instead of Negroes who formerly performed all of this service. The streets are now cleaned by whites, but the asphalt paving is done by Negroes. The longshoremen occupations have remained intact for Negro workers. White men, however, have taken over the scavenger positions with the city. Three years ago Negroes are reported to have laughed when white men were seen digging streets for sewer pipes. It is now the usual thing to see white men doing this work." (Anderson p. 230-231)

This dynamic of the shifts in roles is detailed in "The Proceedings of The South Carolina Historical Association (1981 Columbia, SC). In "Between Two Worlds: Christopher G Memminger of Charleston and the Old South in the Mid-Passage, 1830-1861" written by Laylon Wayne Jordan it reads:

"By far the most important social issue [Christopher G] Memminger addressed and acted upon as a public servant concerned the condition and role, in region, state, and city, of the numerous class of common white people, neither masters nor slaves, who thus did not fit into the traditional ethical and social and economic system of aristocratic paternalism and slave labor. When he first took notice of the matter, in 1849, it was in the context of a newly burgeoning competition between Irish immigrants and free and enslaved blacks for employment in the shops, wharves, and streets of Charleston and the emergence of a public debate over the relative expense and social impact of slaves and free whites as artisans and operatives in factories...In a letter to James Hammond, who strongly favored white labor in an urban context because he apprehended that city employment permitted slaves a dangerous measure of freedom, Memminger expressed a strong contrary fear of white proletariat, with all the supposed implications of moral decay, criminality, and social instability which worried Southern ideologues like Calhoun and Rhett. A free white working class was 'the only party from which danger to our institutions is to be apprehended among us,' he wrote:

Drive out the negro mechanics and all sorts of operaties [sic] from our Cities, and who must take their place[?] The same men who make the cry in the Northern Cities against tyranny of Capital...and would soon raise hue and cry against the Negro, and be hot Abolitionists-and every one of those men would have a vote...The scheme by which...[the most fiendish of abolitionists] has expected to foment division among us is based on this element of Discord.

If Memminger's analysis was close to correct, it followed that Charleston and other Southern cities had open two possible course of action. Conservatives and pro-slavery enthusiasts suggested that the better course was to suppress further immigration and create codes that favored slave over free labor. The approach that Memminger came around to, after it was brilliantly espoused by James Taylor, a pioneer in textile manufacturing in the state, and that Charleston adopted was to assume that the fate of the city, state, and region was inseparable from the fate of the 'vague race lumped together indiscriminately as...poor whites,' that the 'forgotten' people of the South, including the worthy among the immigrants, had the potential for much good as well as evil, and should be cultivated. This line of reasoning led him to undertake what was in some ways his most consequential public career: as the 'father' of modern public schools in Charleston. (p.64-65)

In 1854 Memminger was appointed to the Board of Commissioners of Free Schools in Charleston by the South Carolina Legislature. Children of color, free and slave, were excluded. Common whites did not need education beyond the humblest form because more might make them unfit for their common work.

"In 1867 the Morris Street School for colored children was opened under the aegis of a school board composed of leading white citizens, and by October, 1879, had an enrollment of over a thousand pupils and a daily average attendance of ninety-three per cent. Mary Street School, another graded school for Negroes, had at the same time thirteen teachers and over six hundred pupils. In all there were 3,586 Negro pupils enrolled in Charleston city schools in 1878-1879, and the expenditures in that year were nearly one-fifth as much as those for the entire state system." (Tindall p. 218)

Memminger was in a position of power that allowed him to carry out the wishes of many of the Anglo people. In 1880 the first county teachers' institute for "Negro" teachers was held, but "Negro" teachers were not being hired. As of 1896 there were only two in the entire school system. So, continued pressure came from the community to challenge this.

The fact that the now free people of African descent were acting in accordance with their right to be free, many were offended by this. William Heyward's comments that he made during a visit to the *Charleston Hotel* expressed a permeating sentiment of the time:

" *'I am perfectly independent of having negroes about me; if I cannot have them as they used to be, I have no desire to see them except in the field.' Another contemporary believed it 'revolting' to reside 'in a Land where Free Negroes make the majority of the inhabitants.' This was especially galling because 'every mulattoe [sic] is your equal & every 'Nigger' is your superior.'... One refugee was the prosperous landowner Dr. Arthur G. Rose, who emigrated to England because he 'couldn't stay in a country with so many free negroes'."* (Powers p. 228)

Being clearly aware of the sentiments expressed toward them, Gullah/Geechees gathered at *Morris Brown Church* in November 1855 to call for an end to

251

interracial violence. There had been a number of attacks and murders that had taken place. Thus, the ministers were called upon to issue an address to the races.

It laid out the accomplishments and progress that the "Negro" had already made. It then ended with the following warning:

"It is openly said that this is a 'white man's government,' and the negro must be kept down. We must warn the white people in time. They may go on depriving us of our rights until forbearance ceases to be a virtue. It may not be long before the revolutions of St. Domingo in the times of Toussaint L'Overture will be repeated in the South..."

Such a warning no doubt had to be seriously considered given that people of African descent occupied all areas of Charleston during Reconstruction and well into the latter 1900s when gentrification and gated areas truly began major displacement of the families. According to Dr. Bernard E. Powers' *"Black Charlestonians"*:

"In 1880 blacks continued to be widely distributed through every part of the city and nothing resembling the modern urban ghetto existed. Certain closely settled enclaves of black population had begun to emerge however. The descriptive popular names some- times applied to certain streets with large numbers of black residents provide illustrative testimony to this fact. For in- stance, Beresford Alley was commonly known as Mulatto Alley, and a section of Philadelphia Street was pejoratively referred to as Coon Alley. A contemporary pamphlet described the area of King Street between Battery and Queen Street (in ward two) as 'in- fested by' negroes. Part of this area was destroyed by the disastrous fire of 1861 and still remained 'one of the most dis- agreeable and dirty portions of the city.' In this vicinity, Smith's Lane, Wimm's Court, and Price's Alley, which ran perpendicular to King Street just north of the Battery, were overwhelmingly inhabited by black residents. Generally, clusters of black population tended to be east or west of ten north-south corridor formed by Meeting and King Streets. Princess, Beresford, Clifford's Alley, Simon's Row, and several other streets in ward two west of King Street between Beaufain and Queen were also heavily populated by blacks. In the lower wards, the black population gravitated toward the numerous alleyways, lanes, and courts that bisected the larger streets. This was especially the case in the eastern portion of wards one and three where blacks were concentrated in residences behind the wharves. Stoll's Alley, St. Michael's Alley, and Cordes Court were typical, and the residences here were inhabited largely by blacks employed as domestics, laborers, cotton hands, fishermen, pilots, sailors, and longshoremen.

The sections of the city where blacks concentrated were not only unaesthetic but also quite often unhealthy. This was certainly the case in the northeastern portion of ward three, which was bounded by Calhoun, Anson, and Laurens. This area was known as Gadsdenboro or, more descriptively, as Rottenborough. Largely inhabited by working class blacks, according to the board of health, this part of the city had long been regarded 'with indignant disgust' by the community. The area was almost entirely comprised of low land and marsh land. Attempts were made to fill this low-lying district with street sweepings, sawdust, rice chaff, offal, and dirt, but decomposition ensued, and the land sank down again.

During periods of heavy rain, the land flooded, and stagnant pools collected under the houses, which caused the board of health to describe this area as a "dangerous and un-healthy region" that served as a breeding ground for infectious diseases. The conditions that obtained here occurred in many places on the east side and were avoided by all who could afford residences in more salubrious locations.

The upper wards were generally less healthy than the lower part of the city. The land along the Ashley and Cooper rivers were quite low and especially so in ward seven, which was criss-crossed with rivulets. During high tides and periods of heavy rain, the land became inundated. The drainage network was adequate in many places, which made it difficult to maintain sanitary conditions. Garbage was formerly dumped in Charleston Neck and used to reclaim land, and human excrement continued to be deposited at the northern end of King and Meeting streets. Many residents believed that the poor sanitary conditions in the upper wards were responsible for the incidence of malarial fevers and a related ailment popularly known as Neck Fevers.

A major trend occurring during

Reconstruction and the years thereafter was the gradual shift of the black population north-ward. In 1860 9,728 or 58.6 percent, of all Charleston's blacks resided in the lower four wards, but by 1880, although their absolute number had increased to 11,848, only 45.6 percent of all blacks continued to reside there. Seven of the city's eight wards reflected increased black populations during the twenty-year period, but the black population was expanding much more rapidly in the upper wards. While the percent increase in wards five through eight varied between 75 and 187 percent, a growth rate of 55 percent was the greatest registered by any of the lower four wards. The northwestern part of the upper city was growing quite rapidly as low-lying lots were filled in, and farm land was sold for building sites. By 1880 blacks made up 60 and 62 percent of wards six and eight respectively, and these two wards became the site for one of the largest concentrations of blacks in the city. At this time, the area west and north of the railroad yards and workshops between Vanderhorst and Congress, including Warren, Radcliffe, Morris, Bogard, Race, Chestnut, Fludd, and a number of nearby streets were heavily settled by blacks. Quite often, the male workers of this area were employed as laborers, farm hands, mill hands, and to a lesser extent as craftsmen. Though concentrations of blacks are discernible, they were not confined to these areas, and most lived in other locations. At this time, class was as important a determinant of residential pattern as race was." (p.250)

As time went on, communities were built throughout the peninsula. Many of them were near the major parks were families and residents would gather such as Harmon Field on Fishburne Street, Martin Park at the corner of Lee and America Street, and another park that was bounded by Calhoun, Concord, and Washington Streets.

Many of these areas around the peninsula have been greatly impacted by gentrification which has been brought on due to increased tourism and the expansion of the colleges. The changing dynamics in construction have caused a consistent process of displacement of businesses of people of African descent as well as families from the downtown area.

The *St. James Hotel* that was built in fall 1951 at the corner of Spring Street and Hagood Avenue was first the first hotel for Blacks. It was operated by four Washington Brothers. They also owned *Ashley Grill* which was the largest black owned restaurant at that time. The Cation Brothers also operated a restaurant downtown during the early 1900. *Gullah Cuisine* in Mount Pleasant and Savannah's on Highway 17 just outside of West Ashley have continued this restaurant tradition. In addition to these businesses, *Lincoln Theater* which was owned by David I. Thomas was only black owned theater on King Street near Spring Street.

Just as many of these businesses have faded from the pages of Charleston history, many of the communities that served to nurture Gullah/Geechees that had sought to make a life for themselves there. The communities of Elliottborough, Canonborough, and Radcliffeborough and Ansonborough which is known as "The Boro" were such places.

"The Boro" which only has two of its original Ansonborough Homes remaining at 35 and 35 1/2 Calhoun Street was an area that truly showed the issues of race in regard to the living patterns of the peninsula. During the 1720s Captain George Anson of the Royal Navy obtained land on the peninsula between

King Street and Cooper River bounded by Hassell, Meeting, George, Laurens, and East Bay Streets. The original homes that were built along this major "slave entry" point on the peninsula were destroyed when a fire swept through in 1838.

During Reconstruction, Ansonborough was an industrial area. This time the trade items were lumber and creosote instead of people. This area became one of housing for many of those that would work to get these products out to the rest of the country. The *S. M. Parker Lumber Company* had buildings in this area during the 1880s. In particular, "rosin yards" and sheds were housed there. Rosin was used in the caulking of ships as well as to make varnishes. During the 1930s, the *Charleston Steel and Metal Company* and the *Charleston Shipbuilding & Dry Dock Company* operated from this area as well. The *Charleston Gas Light Company* operated in this area until the August 3, 1886 earthquake. This earthquake caused extensive damage to their entire system of operation. Numerous homeless Gullah/Geechee gathered in a tent city in Marion and Washington squares for months after this. Many of the buildings in Charleston that remained standing have metal rods running through them today. These are to assist in stabilizing the buildings in the event of another earthquake.

From cotton to electricity has been processed through "The Boro." The creosote that was processed here was used to preserve wood. At one point, it was also utilized in disinfectants and health cures as well. During Reconstruction some of the people that came from plantations on the islands and outer lying areas, made their way to the city to work in the industries that were there. As the years went on, people continued to come and raise their families in this area of the peninsula.

Many did not want to leave the islands, but found themselves with no other recourse when lands were restored to those that had abandoned it. In 1866, many freedmen died from exposure waiting at Steamboat Landing to fulfill and evacuation order from Edisto. They were sent away so that the land could be returned to former plantation owners and enslavers. Churches were even taken back from the Gullah/Geechees that had been congregating there. The fact that it was their hands that originally built these buildings was not taken into account. It was simply about "ownership."

Many plantations were left behind by Gullah/Geechees throughout the area. Rebecca Campbell and Catherine Braxton trace their family heritage back to Drayton Hall prior to their family planting their roots at the remaining buildings of "The Boro." Their grandfather, Wilis Bowen Johnson bought land in "The Boro" in 1939. He sold his piece on Concord Street to the city so that the coming "housing project" could be built. He then took some of the money and purchased the buildings at 35 and 35 1/2 Calhoun Street.

In 1940 162 units for a "housing project" for "Blacks" was built in Ansonborough. The boundaries of the project were Washington, Calhoun, Concord, and Laurens Streets. These brick one-story row houses with hollow tile walls, concrete floors, and old Charleston tile roofs were built low to the ground which meant that with every rain, the families felt the flood. The community endured what they had to and continued to work and even begin their own businesses. This became a true community and not just a "project" as it had been outlined by the United States Federal Government funding documents.

The Wragg Borough Homes had been built three blocks north of Ansonborough. There were 128 units were built between South, Drake, Chapel, and Alexander Streets. However, they were found to be of inferior quality. The Ansonborough Homes started renting at $1.75 a week for a 3 1/2 bedroom to $2.80 per week for a five 1/2 room which included lights and water. The executive director of the housing authority stated that these were the lowest rents for decent modern homes that had ever been achieved.

The price for constructing these homes was no doubt kept low because the land in that area was not seen as an "ideal place" to live given the industry that had been and was there. It was a couple of generations before anyone truly examined what "laid beneath the surface" in all of this.

Just as with the great storm of 1893, in 1989 Hurricane Hugo came through Charleston and brought down a lot of things and brought other things to the surface. Numerous areas that had been built up as places of luxury came down in the winds and rains of this storm. Many homes were destroyed and lives were lost. Parts of Charleston County would never look the same again and this storm would never be forgotten.

As Hugo's waters sat in Ansonborough, many people were trapped in their homes for days. Although the storm did not take away the only home that many of the people there had known, the city had a different idea.

In 1990 the housing authority had a report done which showed that there were toxic deposits of benzo-a-prene (a cancer causing agent) in the soil where the Ansonborough Homes stood. It was not deem dangerous other than through ingestion. The fact that people raised their children here and the children played in the playground where these deposits could have infiltrated the soil was part of the reasoning for closing the dwellings. Although the *Environmental Protection Agency* (EPA) was brought in to oversee the removal of affected sediments on surrounding land, the community members were not allowed to move back after the buildings were demolished. This area is rapidly becoming the hub of tourism activity and condominiums which has caused the community to continue to be outraged about the displacement. The *Charleston Post & Courier* captured the sentiments in 1996 when they printed a brief piece on Ansonborough and wrote:

"All this has disappeared, the houses, the smells, the cries and the people, yet the memories live on amongst those who lived there and played there. It was not an easy life growing up in the Borough, as many residents have stated but what remains true to their experience is that children were allowed to be children and the whole village was responsible for raising a child in the neighborhood. The concern for family respect extended beyond the nucleus family and involved neighbors and extended families. The demolition of the Ansonborough Homes was the end to a particular way of life of which African Americans in Charleston had created against tremendous adversity to be integrated."

Questions remain as to whether or not the "health threat" was just a ploy that added to the history of adversity of this community. Many are not sure if it was not simply a part of a greater plan to remove the people of African descent from the "public eye" as people come and visit the city that has become known as the "most hospitable city in America" since it won this recognition several years in the running.

Running is what many of the Gullah/Geechees of Charleston have found themselves continually doing as they seek a place to settle down and stay for multiple generations. The Eastside Community members and many others have found themselves having to relocate to North Charleston and West Ashley in order to find an affordable place to live as Charleston continues to boom amidst the many growing cities of the Gullah/Geechee Nation.

The *International African American Museum (IAAM)* that will stand in the Ansonborough community seeks to be a living monument that will provide people with insights into the stories of the Gullah/Geechees and other Africans of the Diaspora and what was built as a result of their knowledge and wherewithal. The entire city of Charleston is already one such monument that many people walk through and walk over without truly being educated about all that has occurred there. If one wants to learn of the foundations of America, all they need to do is stop and take in a few lessons in Charleston.

Fa Lurn Wi

Whether education or miseducation was what Gullah/Geechees received is in the eye of the beholder. "Training" into a particular way of thinking may be a more adequate term for the various processes that were put forth under the guise of education over the years given that most of it contributed to generations of Gullah/Geechees being taught to deny their African heritage. The process of stripping the Africans of their actual names, their languages, their traditions, and spiritual practices were all part of a system of indoctrination that needed to be put in place in order to take a group of human beings and convince them that they were no longer people, but simply slaves; to take groups of people of African descent and convince them that they were "niggers" even though they were the ones that were being enslaved in order to have them work (Webster initially defined the word "nigger" as a "lazy, shiftless individual"); to give a group that consist of a number of ethnic groups one name and then when they take on the name (as in the case of Gullah or Geechee) to get them to believe that it means that they are "backwards" and "ignorant" instead of the truth that they descended from a particular place in Africa and the list goes on. The institutions of this process took on varying forms from the colonial years to the present times.

When Africans were first enslaved in North America, there were no rules against them reading or writing. This restriction came as a result of major uprisings such as the "Stono Rebellion." One of the major gathering locations for the Africans to educate themselves on how to take back their freedom was in the "bush arbors" and "brush arbors." Thus, infiltrating the spiritual spheres was a major mechanism for controlling what thoughts would be transmitted throughout the plantations.

"The *Society for the Propagation of the Gospel in Foreign Parts*" was founded in London in 1701 as a missionary arm of the Church of England to minister to the colonists of America and also to instruct the Indians and Negroes. They focused mainly on children and made slow progress as they gained permission from "slave owners" to catechize the enslaved Africans. Samuel Thomas of Goose Creek was one of the first *S.P.G.* missionaries sent to South Carolina. Alexander Garden, a native of Scotland who arrived in 1719 was appointed rector of St. Philip's Parish and in

1726 he became the commissioner for North and South Carolina and the Bahama Islands. As the bishop of the London commissary in South Carolina, he suggested that schools be established, but that the instruction be conducted "by Negro Schoolmasters, Home-born, & equally Property as other Slaves, but educated for this Service, & employed in it during their Lives, as the others are in any other Service whatsoever." The society ended up purchasing Harry and Andrew when they were 14 and 15 and trained them to be teachers. They had been baptized as infants.

"Garden's School for Negroes was opened on September 12, 1743, and lasted over twenty years, despite the fact that in 1740 the South Carolina Legislature, in reaction to the Stono Rebellion of 1739, had adopted a strict law against teaching slaves to write. In 1746 Garden informed the society that the school had already trained twenty-eight children and was at that time instructing fifty-five more children during the day and fifteen adults in the evening. The type of education offered can be inferred from Garden's request to the society for the following books: 100 Spelling Books, 50 Testaments, 50 Bibles, and 50 Psalters with Common Prayer.

The aim of the Charlestown Negro School was stated clearly by Commissary Garden in his letter of 1740:

> As among us Religious Instruction usually descends from Parents to Children, so among them it must at first ascend from Children to Parents, or from young to Old.
>
> They are as 'twere a Nation within a Nation. In all County Settlements, they live in contiguous Houses and often 2, 3, or 4 Familys of them in one House, Slightly partitioned into so many Apartments. They labour together and converse almost wholly among themselves, so that if once their children could but read the Bible to them, and other Tracts of Instruction of Evenings & other spare Times, specially Sundays; would bring in at least a Dawning of the blessed Light amongst them; and which as a Sett or two of these children grew up to Men and Women, would gradually diffuse and increase into open Day." ("Slave Religion" p. 116)

Garden had died in 1756. The Charlestown school closed in 1764 when Harry died. Andrew had proved a profligate as evidenced in the following account:

"The [SC] Society says that in 1752 a flourishing negro school was taught in Charlestown by a negro who worked under the inspection and direction of the Society official, and many negroes were taught the Christian culture. It was considered that to be baptized was inconsistent with a state of slavery. To obviate this difficulty, South Carolina passed an Act declaring it lawful for any negro to receive and profess the Christian faith and to be baptized, but they did not thereby become freemen.

The Rev. Mr. Taylor, in 1713, examined a number of negroes in St Andrew's Parish, who received instruction through Mrs. Haig and Mrs. Edwards. Rev. Mr. Garden had a schoolhouse for negroes built in Charlestown and for twenty-one years a number of children, varying from thirty to sixty, in number, with sometimes as many as fifteen adults were instructed there. Other schools were organized and churches erected for the colored population, and their religious instruction became a matter of great consideration with all the Christian denominations." (Leiding p.67-68)

Other groups that did begin their own groups in order to socialize and later to educate themselves were the "*Brown Fellowship Society*" that started in 1790 and "*The Humane and "Friendly Society."* The *Humane* was started in 1802 and the Friendly Union began in 1818 which led to the *Friendly Moralist*, *Brotherly Association*, and the *Unity and Friendship* group. Each had their own burial lot and mutual aid societies.

Humane Brotherhood "further resolved 'that we, free dark men of the City of Charleston, do form ourselves into a Compact Body for the purpose of alleviating each other in sickness and death.' Although it also declared 'that this Society shall exclusively supported by any number of free, dark men,..'" ("Black Charlestonians" p.296)

"The *Brown Fellowship Society* was organized as a voluntary association with motto 'Charity and Benevolence' by free Afro- Americans who belonged to the white *St. Philip's Episcopal Church,* where they worshipped, were baptized and married but could not be interred in its burial ground. The preamble to its rules and regulations explained its existence because of the 'unhappy situation of our fellow creatures, and the distress of our widows and orphans, for want of a fund to relieve them in the hour of their distress, sickness, and death.' It is most likely that the founders of the *Brown Fellowship Society* selected that name to distinguish themselves from the 'Fellow- ship Society,' a white voluntary association formed some thirty years earlier. ("Charleston's Free Afro-American Elite: The Brown Fellowship Society and the Humane Brotherhood." p. 292)

As time went on, *Brown Fellowship* membership was limited to 50 men over 21. Each paid $50 dues. They were entitled to benefits if disabled and burial if they did not leave sufficient means in their estates for this.

Social purity and loyalty were the "capstones" of the society. George Logan was put out of the *Brown Fellowship* when it was confirmed that he was in collusion with having a free black man named Robinson sold as a slave.

The "social purity" was generally maintained through only allowing "mulattoes" to gain membership. "In 1860, seventy-five percent of Charleston's free Black community was mulatto, while only eight percent of the entire county's free Blacks were mulatto." (p. 10 Van Houten, Abigail "The Preservation of Freedmen's Cottages as a Physical Representation of African American History and Culture" Senior Thesis 2000) "The ratio of colored men to women in the city was approximately 2 to 3 in 1861. Slaves that lived on the plantations shared a more even gender balance thus experiencing less family instability than city dwellers. The imbalance increased the number of Black women who intermingled with white men producing a larger number of mulatto children." (Abigail p. 9)

"One of the twenty-four members whose color was determined, however, was categorized in the 1860 federal census as black. That was Malcolm Brown who joined the *Brown Fellowship* in 1828 and whose father, Morris Brown, had been forced to leave the state in 1822 after the Denmark Vesey Conspiracy. Malcolm Brown with his father and five other free Afro-Americans had been trustees of the African Society which purchased a lot in 1818 to erect a building for an *African Methodist Episcopal (AME) Church*. The congregation, both slave and free, had 1,848 members in 1818, making the Charleston AME Church the second largest in the United States, behind Philadelphia with 3,311, but ahead of Baltimore with 1,066, which also had a much larger free Afro-American population. Because several suspected leaders of the Vesey Conspiracy were officials of the AME Church, Charleston public authorities made the congregation disband and demolished its church building. This episode ended the city's independent black church movement until after the Civil War. It also made free Afro-Americans in general more circumspect in their activities to avoid suspicion." ("Charleston's Free Afro-American Elite: The Brown Fellowship Society and the Humane Brotherhood." p. 292-293)

The groups tended to keep their gatherings low key. One of the prime meeting places of free Blacks was Coming Street on the peninsula.

People of African descent tend to have large gatherings for homegoings or funeral services. The societies wanted to insure that these rites were properly carried out and that their dead had places to be interred. Thus, the *Brown Fellowship* first had its cemetery at Pitt Street near where the *College of Charleston* is now. In 1940

Bishop England Catholic School bought the land. In 1957 the school needed more space for parking and purchased more land. 88 Smith Street became the new *Brown Fellowship* location.

Friendly Union Society began its cemetery in 1813. Unity and Friendship Cemetery is off Meeting Road was founded in the early 1800s. Thomas Smalls was a wealthy dark skinned man that established the Brotherly Cemetery in 1843 to have a society where he and others of his complexion would be welcome.

As always, organizations continued to be founded to suit specific purposes. "In 1803, seven *Brown Fellowship* men started the *Minor's Moralist Society* to support and to educate indigent and orphaned colored children." (The South Carolina Historical Magazine 1981 Vol. 82 No. 4 Charleston, SC "Charleston's Free Afro-American Elite: The Brown Fellowship Society and the Humane Brotherhood." p.295) James Mitchell, Joseph Humphries, William Cooper, Carlos Huger, Thomas S. Bonneau, William Clark, and Richard Holloway were all affluent free colored men. They wanted to provide for the needs and necessary wants of these children.

The *Minor's Moralist Society* consisted of fifty members, who contributed five dollars each at first, and paid thereafter the monthly sum of twenty-five cents each. As many as six children were at one time receiving care and attention because of the contributions of these men. The organization continued in existence until 1847, when, from the decease of many useful members and other local causes, it ceased to exist.

The *Christian Benevolent Society* was another organization created to cope with the problem of indigence among free blacks. Organized in 1839, according to the members, its purpose was 'the commiseration and aid of the sick poor of our free Colored Community of the City, by pecuniary grants, and Judicious Council.' From its inception until 1856, the organization spent $1,228 and aided seventy persons.

Daniel Alexander Payne was an orphan that became an African Methodist Episcopal Bishop that attended the Minor's Moralist Society and later open an academy for free Afro-American youth in Charleston. He had 60 pupils at one point, but was forced to close the school in 1835 due to the prohibition of free persons of color teaching reading and writing to other Negroes in SC. He left the state after the law came into affect. Francis Pinckney Holloway was a free Black in Charleston that operated a school for free blacks. Francis also left due to threats to his school and his person.

The *Society of Free Dark Men* was formed also. Some say it was due to rifts concerning barring people with questionable morals such as women who were seen openly with white men. Thomas Small was the founder. He wanted to avoid the color discrimination of the *Brown Fellowship*. Both associations' burial areas were on Pitt Street separated only by a fence.

They dynamics of these organizations are easily reflected when looking at a roster of their members:

Brown Fellowship Members: Malcolm Brown, John Deledge, Joseph and Richard Dereef (Indian in census), James F Hatt, Richard and Charles Holloway, Thomas Holmes, Richard Kinloch, James Maxwell, William McKinlay, Joseph Sasportas (white man to a Haitian woman), William Seymour, and Jacob Weston

Humane Brotherhood Members: Nelson Anderson, Moses and William Berry,

William Emmerly, William Jackson, Peter Mazyck, William Mitchell, Paul Poinsett, Richard and Thomas Small

Owned slaves: Malcolm Brown, Richard Dereef, Richard Holloway, Richard Kinloch, James Maxwell, William McKinlay, and William Seymour

Occupations: Tailor, Carpenter, Shoemaker, Barber, Hairdresser, Fisherman, Millwright, Tinner, Wheelwright, Bricklayer, Drayman, Sexton, Hotelkeeper, Drummer, Butcher, Tavernkeeper, Woodfactor, Planter

36 free Afro-American males owned 99 African people that they enslaved.

Abraham Jones was expelled from Brown and became a member of Humane. He was married at the *St. Philip's Episcopal Church*. Paul Poinsett also married there and Edward Logan baptized his children there. "After the Civil War, at least four Brown Fellowship men left the white Methodist Episcopal Church which demanded that they continue to sit segregated in the gallery. They established *Centenary Methodist Episcopal Church* in 1866, while five of their cohorts had already left St. Philip's in 1865 to form *St. Mark's Episcopal Church*." ("Black Charlestonians" p. 304)

"The *Brown Fellowship Society* [started in 1790] and the Humane Brotherhood [started in 1843] were undoubtedly the two most important organizations extant among Charleston's free Afro-American elite during the 1840s." (The South Carolina Historical Magazine (c) 1981 Vol. 82 No. 4 Charleston, SC) The elite all had their special private gatherings many times along Coming Street. As the organizations grew, there were women's auxillaries as well. These eventually grew into the *"Charleston Federation of Colored Women's Clubs."*

"The *Phyllis Wheatley Club* members ended up being Charleston elites. Mrs. Cox the founder looked to have "a mixture of a perfect social compound. Culture was to be the means to unite black leadership and to foster racial solidarity to create a truly 'united, homogeneous Negro society'." (The Proceedings of The South Carolina Historical Association 1998 p.42)

Later on other civic groups and social clubs that continue to exist in Charleston would come about. Amongst them are members of what started out in 1867 to be the *"South Carolina Grand Lodge of Negro Freemasons."* The Freemasons had their own forms of initiation processes that had originally come from the Kemetic (or Egyptian) secret society traditions. These have greatly changed over the years as did the focus of the groups or lodges.

"Nathan I Huggins has written that mulatto Saint Domingue refugees 'flocked into the southern port cities of Charleston, Savannah, Mobile, and New Orleans, bringing with them both the anxieties of a violently displaced people and expectations that a social system of three castes-white, black, and mulatto-would continue. Charleston's mulattoes, according to E Horace Fitchett, formed exclusive associations that separated them from other free Afro-Americans in that city. He explained that 'they came to occupy a position between the masses of Negroes, on the one hand and the white inhabitants on the other hand.

Their accommodation to such a position seemed to protect them from some of the most oppressive techniques of control. Hence, this treatment tended to give this group a superior conception of itself." ("Charleston's Free Afro-American Elite: The Brown Fellowship Society and the Humane Brotherhood." p. 289)

In a memorial to a state governor on January 10, 1861, "Free Blacks of Charleston" made their position clear in regard to where their loyalties were when their representative stated:

"In our veins flows the blood of the white race, in some half, in others much more than half white blood...our attachments are with you, our hopes and safety and protection from you...our allegiance is due to South Carolina and in her defense, we will offer up our lives, and all that is dear to us."

Even this honest plea did not gain acceptance as equals for most of the mulattos. There were those that chose to leave the area and then "pass" as Anglo people in other places. Others continued to strive for ways to achieve their acceptance. Many did and continue to attempt to gain acceptance from "education." Whether or not they use what they learn to simply benefit themselves or to benefit "the race" is a good indicator of their initial motivations.

In spite of the fact that in 1834 there was a law to prohibit the education of enslaved Africans and to greatly restrict the education of "free Negroes," there were at least fifteen schools operated for this purpose and were run by "free Negroes." A number of native Charlestonians utilized their education to take them to other parts of the world where what they wanted to contribute would be accepted. Francis L. Cardozo was a freeborn mulatto that was the son of a prominent Charleston economist and editor. Cardozo attended the *University of Glasgow* and studied theology in Edinburgh and London and then returned to the United States. He pastored the *Temple Street Congregational Church* in New Haven, CT. However, after Charleston fell, he came back home to be the principal of a Negro school operated by the *American Missionary Association (AMA)*.

Cardozo had a negative expectation of black teachers. He placed whites in higher positions. When he was confronted, he tried to justify this by saying that this was only due to competence. He also chose freeborn blacks over previously enslaved in regard to enrollment. He made students go home that did not pay their tuition right away. Thus, the school gradually became more and more exclusive.

Cardozo did stand for black rights and warn against "treacherous whites" that were seeking to regain political control of the state. He eventually went to the state convention himself since people felt that he should due to the fact that he was educated. November 1865 *Zion Church* hosted a colored people's convention. Robert C. De Large, A. J. Ransier, J. J. Wright, Beverly Nash, Francis L. Cardozo, M. R. Delany, and Richard H. Cain were all a part of it.

Although many mulattos had the opportunity to be educated during the plantation era, many of the enslaved Gullah/Geechees were not afforded this opportunity openly until the Civil War began. Most of the schools that were started at that time were run by northern missionary associations like the *AMA*.

On Edisto Island, the school system was to be headed by James Pierpoint Blake. He was the grand nephew of Eli Whitney. Blake could not serve in the war since he had been crippled by polio as a child. Thus, he thought that educating the freedmen would be a way that he could serve his country and he joined in with the *New England Missionary Society*. He was first sent to Beaufort, SC and then on to Edisto.

On Edisto, Blake worked with Mary Ames,

Emily Bliss, and Nicholas Balisdell at Crawford's. Ellen Kempton and Elmira Stanton established a school at Middleton's on the island. These women shared the big house at this plantation with the freedmen. Mrs. Webb, the wife of a lieutenant, also opened a school at the Army Headquarters. Mr. Everett and Blake opened a school at "Murray Plantation" as well. Blake was the superintendent of these schools. However, the most successful school on the island was run by a minister of the baptist church. In the years since, the islanders have had the school district name schools in honor of their own people including the *Jane Edwards School* on the island. Ms. Edwards gave many years of service in teaching at *The Borough School* on the island.

Schools for Negroes after the fall of Charleston opened at noon and closed at three due to field work. In spite of these short days, there were many native Charlestonians that not only took full advantage of these opportunities to learn, they also proceeded in making history themselves.

R. L. Smith was a native of Charleston that founded the *Farmers' Improvement Society*. He eventually moved to Texas and there he became the principal of the *Oakland Texas Normal School*. He was also a politician who was elected to the Texas Legislature in 1894 and 1896 in a predominantly white district.

Benjamin Brawley of *Morehouse* and *Howard Universities* was the son of a Charleston minister. *Howard University*'s campus was one of many through which Dr. Ernest Everett just strolled.

Ernest Everett Just was a true scholar. He sought to find "truth" using scientific methods and inquiry. Although Dr. Just was bold enough to challenge the theories of leading biologists of the 19th and 20th centuries, he was humble and unassuming. Dr. Just was passionately driven to understand the world of the cell. His tenacity and motivation led him to add to our understanding of the process of artificial parthenogenesis and the physiology of cell development.

Dr. Just was born August 14, 1883 in Charleston, South Carolina to Charles and Mary Just. The couple also later had Hunter and Inez join the family. The Just Family lived through the Charleston earthquake unlike many others that were around them.

The miracles in Just's life would

continue even after the storm. The Just Family moved to James Island because their house on the peninsula was damaged. They established their new home in the area called "Maryville." As young Ernest went around the island, he demonstrated a gift for academic research and took an interest in his environment. He attended school every day, but his mother felt that he could have a better quality of education in the north. Thus, she sought information and eventually applied for a scholarship for Ernest at the *Kimball Academy* in Meridien, New Hampshire.

The family waited for quite some time to hear back from the school. Being eager to expand his horizons, Ernest went north to visit the school. He was 17 years old when he took a ship to New York. He was able to work on the ship in order to pay for his fare. Once he arrived at his destination he had $5 and two pairs of shoes. He marched up to *Kimball Academy* and found out that he had won the scholarship!

Just graduated in three years instead of four. He was at the top of the 1903 graduating class. This led to him receiving a scholarship to *Dartmouth College* in Hanover, New Hampshire. In 1907, he was the only person to graduate magna cum laude from Dartmouth College with a degree in zoology, special honors in botany and history, and honors in sociology.

Immediately after graduation, Dr. Just taught at Howard University where he was appointed head of the Department of Zoology in 1912. Also, on June 26, 1912 he married Ethel Highwarden who was a teacher. They had three children, Margaret, Highwarden, and Maribel.

At Howard, Just also served as a professor in the medical school and head of the Department of Physiology until his death. The first *Spingarn Medal* was awarded to the reluctant and modest Just by the *NAACP* in 1915 for his accomplishments as a pure scientist. In 1916, Dr. Just graduated magna cum laude from *University of Chicago* receiving his doctorate in experimental embryology.

Dr. Just received international acclaim for work he completed during the summers from 1909 to 1930 at the *Marine Biological Laboratory* (MBL) in Woods Hole, Massachusetts. At MBL, he conducted thousands of experiments studying the fertilization of the marine mammal cell. In 1922, he successfully challenged Jacque Loeb's theory of artificial parthenogenesis, pushing the envelope. Using his research conducted at Wood's Hole, he published his first book entitled, Basic Methods for Experiments on Eggs of Marine Mammals.

Although Dr. Just was considered a leader and authority for his work with cell development, as a person of African descent, he experienced racism and prejudice. For this reason, Dr. Just decided to study in Europe in 1930. It was in Europe that he published his second book, The Biology of the Cell Surface. While in Europe in 1938 he published a number of papers and lectured on the topic of cell cytoplasm. Dr. Just died October 27, 1941 in Washington D.C. He left behind sixty papers and two books about his work. However, many that walk the streets of Charleston have never heard of his accomplishments. There is a small plaque located at his birthplace in the Ansonborough community in his honor. Given the position of the plaque and its size, many visitors through the city will never stop and pay homage to this great man because the marker is not easily seen.

Many others such as Martin R. Delany, Benjamin A. Boseman, and Ingliss are not often heard of outside of academic arenas and writings of today. These were some of the men that received "appointed" positions of leadership after the attempts to head from Reconstruction to Jim Crow began to take its toll on the political machine. Delany was a trial justice, Boseman was a postmaster, and Ingliss was the jury commissioner for Charleston County.

Having the world see that people of African descent did have knowledge and could create a myriad of things was often the focal point of public exhibitions and the like. "On the banks of the Ashley River a little north of Charleston was the SC Interstate and West Indian Exposition which only remained open six months. One of the three dozen attractions was the Negro Building. It was erected "to illustrate the marvelous industrial and commercial development of the Southern States in the last quarter of a century, and to contribute to the expansion of American commerce in other lands and among the islands of the Southern seas, specifically, the Exposition was held to inaugurate new commercial industries, to keep open foreign markets-especially in the West Indies, to develop the silk and tea industry, to promote southern manufacturers of cotton and iron, to establish new steamship lines from Charleston, and to promote the port of Charleston." ("Blacks and the South Carolina Interstate and West Indian Exposition" p.211)

The "South Carolina Interstate and West Indian Exposition opened on December 1, 1901 and the doors closed six months later. At the Natural Section near the Louisiana Purchase Building and the Guatemala Building was the "Negro Building." Dr. W.[iliiam] D.[emosthenes] Crum[collector of the Charleston Port who later resigned], a Republican Party leader, who was born a free man in Charleston attended *Avery Normal Institute* and graduated in 1875. He then went on to study at *Howard University* and graduated from the medical school at 1880. In 1883 he married the daughter of escapees, William and Ellen Craft, Ellen Craft of London. By 1900 he was the head of the black hospital, and active AME, a trustee at Avery, a local businessman, and an interracial diplomat. He and Thomas J. Jackson, secretary and field assistant, made sure that the Negro department was completed. It had an executive committee which included Booker T. Washington as the chief commissioner, and Dr. Thomas E.

Miller, the President of SC State (the State Colored College of Orangeburg). The assistant commissioners were E. A. Lawrence, S. W. Bennett, William Ingliss, W. J. Parker, the Reverend N. B. Sterett, and the Reverend J. L. Dart." (Smyth "Blacks and the South Carolina Interstate and West Indian Exposition" p. 211)

The bureaus of the Negro Department were agriculture, art and sculpture, manufacturers run by T. W. Thurston, manager of the Ashley and Bailey Silk Mill in Fayetteville, North Carolina and transportation, horticulture and fruit, history, minerals and forestry, medicine, dentistry, and hygiene run by Dr. Robert J. Macbeth and, education run by Kelly Miller of *Howard University*, promotion and publicity, women's was run by Mrs. E. F. Sterrett and was assisted by Mrs. Booker T. Washington, Mrs. M.C. Terrell, Mrs. Daniel Murray, and Mrs. B. K. Bruce, and live- stock. Each was presided over with a three person advisory committee and a superintendent. Reverend M. B. Salter, Thomas Bomar, and A.L. Macbeth also served.

Bradford Lee Gilbert was the chief architect of the Exposition. He placed the building in The Grove amidst live oaks near the racetrack, and automobile speedway, and not far from the Negro restaurant. Dispute over a statue of a woman with cotton on her head, a man and a boy with a banjo had people upset and they called for them to be removed and placed in a main building containing statues instead of having them in front of one of the buildings.

On Thursday, July 4, 1901, the cornerstone of the Negro Building was to be laid. "Black leaders in Charleston organized the event. A parade of Masons, a military band, the colored battalion of the National Guard, schoolchildren, Odd Fellows, Knights of Pythias, Sons of Elect, Good Samaritans, and members of more than six unions preceded by Dr. Crum, the Board of Directors, and J. A. Williams, the Grand Marshal, organized on Coming Street between Calhoun and Cannon Streets. At 4:30 pm the parade marched up Rutledge Avenue to Grove Street. Through the main gate, the civic and military organizations wound around to the site of the Negro Building." (Smyth "Blacks and the South Carolina Interstate and West Indian Exposition" p. 213-214)

January 1, 1902 was declared "Negro Day." A parade was done and *Jenkins*

Orphanage provided music. *Jenkins Orphanage* had a farm several miles north of the city on which children were trained in farming, carpentry, bricklaying, tailoring, shoemaking, cooking, laundering, and dress making. It was largely supported through the work of the *Jenkins Orphanage Band* that often performed on the streets for donations. After the band went to England in 1895 seeking support and returned to Charleston, Jenkins encouraged the city to see that the orphanage kept delinquents off the streets and was thereby providing a viable service. This convinced the city to begin to provide them with funding.

Many people lack knowledge of many organizations that once existed in Charleston and they cannot keep track of the numerous historic events that took place in that city. Thus, "The Museum of the Americas" joined forces with the leaders of the Gullah/Geechee Nation in order to have a 100th year celebration of the South Carolina Interstate and West Indian Exposition in 2001. This outstanding commemoration again brought together people from various areas of the Caribbean and the Gullah/Geechee Nation to examine the historical connections of their lands and to relink in doing trade and cultural exchange with one another. The events took place at the piers, the *South Carolina Aquarium*, Hampton Park, and various other locations around the peninsula.

During the time of the initial exposition, all of the initial displays of the gifts, talents, and intellectual abilities of the law abiding people of African descent throughout the south was not enough to garner acceptance from those that still opposed them rising to the status of being free. "Exclusion from the white mainstream meant that the black community in Charleston had to survive independently. Indeed, blacks started their own newspapers and schools; some joined trade unions and become stevedores. Others worked in knitting mills, cotton mills, shoe factories, and phosphate mines. The number of black lawyers and black doctors multiplied as the community began to turn inward in order to meet its own needs. Many black men and women became teachers in the segregated schools of the state." (The Proceedings of The South Carolina Historical Association p. 37-38)

In 1883 R. L. Smith came forth with the "*Palmetto Press*" weekly newspaper to compete with William Holloway's *"New Era."* These were replaced by the *"Recorder."* This was published by Reverend J. E. Hayne along with *"Hamitic Palladium."* His background as a Baptist minister was most likely where the focus on "Ham's Place in History" came from for the latter publication. Reverend C. W. McCall came from Cheraw, SC with the *"Monitor."* In 1895, Charleston also had the *"Enquirer."*

Some of the most outstanding teachers that came forth took part in the movements to obtain equal rights for all people, especially their own people. On such teacher was Septima Poinsette Clark. She was a native of Charleston born on May 3, 1898. Peter Poinsette, her father, was enslaved on Joel Poinsette farm between the Waccamaw River and Georgetown, SC. Her mother, Victoria Warren Anderson Poinsette, was born in Charleston and taken to Haiti by her uncle in 1864 along with her two sisters, Martha and Maseline. Her mother was a laundress and her father a caterer.

Septima Poinsette graduated from *Avery Normal Institute* with a licentiate of instruction and went to John's Island in 1916 to teach until 1919. "There was only a four-month elementary school on Johns Island when Septima Clark first came over from Charleston to teach as a young teenager in 1916. But few of the island children attended all four months. During harvest season, farmers came and took the children out to help work in the fields. There was no high school for blacks on the island. Some islanders who were fortunate enough to have relatives in Charleston might send their children over to try to get an education there. Nor were there any medical facilities on the island. Islanders had to go to the Jim Crow emergency room in Charleston, where, as one islander recalls, 'the people were treated so badly by the nurses and sometimes the physicians. It was segregated there. And many people died trying to get to medical care.' The islanders carried their peas, corn, potatoes, and rice across to Charleston by rowboat. 'They had a hard time raising their children,' Alice Wine recalled. 'Those old time foreparents was something else, I tell you." (Joyner p. 231)

There were 132 students in the school and she was the teaching principal. In 1919 she went back to Charleston and taught sixth grade at *Avery*.

Poinsette married Nerie Clark in May of 1920. Their daughter died at one month old. However, they also had a son named "Nerie Clark, Jr.".

She returned from Ohio and Columbia to Charleston public school system in 1947 and worked there until 1957. On April 19, 1956, the *South Carolina Legislature* passed a law that stipulated that no city or state employee could be affiliated with a civil rights organization. She refused to hide her affiliations so she lost her job with them including her retirement benefits.

She worked with the *NAACP* to collect signatures in order to get Negro principals in schools. This became a law by the end of that year.

After years of working in Civil Rights, she was elected a member of the Charleston, South Carolina School Board in 1975. The *College of Charleston* awarded her an Honorary Doctorate of Humane Letters in 1978. Her birthplace is now owned by the college. A highway in Charleston and a fountain at "Liberty Square" in front of the *National Park Service's* "Fort Sumter" interpretive center are named in her honor.

Esau Jenkins was taught by Septima Clark on Johns Island. She taught him to read at age 14. Mr. Jenkins and Ms. Clark started the first citizenship education school in 1957. Bernice Robinson was the first teacher there. The major goal of the school was to make islanders aware of their rights as citizens and aware of how to achieve them.

"In January of that year [1957], Bernice Robinson, a cousin of Septima Clark, began the first Citizenship School. Classes were held in an old, dilapidated school building on John's Island bought for $1,500 and fixed up in the front to look like a store. Robinson taught her fourteen students-three men and eleven women-two nights a week for two hours each night. Classes ran through February, the end of the laying-by season. ***

The next year, classes met in December, January, and February. Many people wanted to sign up for them. Word spread to Wadmalaw Island, and Esau Jenkins's daughter Ethel started a class there. Soon, Robinson was supervising five schools on the islands. Other schools opened in Accabee, Charleston Heights, and in the Citizens' Committee Office on Cannon Street." (Smyth p. 113)

By 1960 nearly 600 more blacks were added as registered voters to the rolls of Charleston County. Schools developed on Wadmalaw, Edisto, and in northern parts of Charleston.

Ernest Tobias Felder was one of the tireless workers of the Civil Rights Movement in Charleston. She worked on trainings and meetings with Dr. Martin Luther King, Jr. on his visits to Charleston. Ms. Felder has been awarded the highest honor that the State of South Carolina issues to an individual- the Palmetto Award-for her years of service. She continues to serve as a member of the Wisdom Circle Council of Elders for the Gullah/Geechee Nation and has continued to march from civil rights to human rights.

From the sands of the Sea Islands came spirituals such as "Keep Your Hands on the Plow." As their Gullah/Geechee ancestors had done, the people of these islands took their seeds and planted them deeply in the ground and nurtured a spirit of freedom. They knew that the many battles against those that wanted to up- root those seeds could be distracting so over time the words of that spiritual evolved into one that kept people marching during the 1960s, "Keep Your Eyes on the Prize." Just as this song came from Johns Island and moved across America, so would the Gullah/Geechee seeds spread and with them would spread the stories and energy of a people that had moved from simply accepting what others taught about them to standing as true "grassroots scholars" that had learned that freedom was and is their right!

From Civil to Human Rights

"...it inspires us with hope when we reflect, that our cause is not alone the cause of four millions of black men in this country, but we are intensely alive to the fact that it is also the cause of millions of oppressed men in other 'parts of God's beautiful eart,' who are now struggling to be free in the fullest sense of the word, and God and nature are pledged to their triumph."

These words written in November of 1865 at the Black/Colored People's Convention at *Zion Presbyterian Church* in Charleston still ring truth. However, the truth was too powerful for many to withstand. In fact, one Anglo-Carolinian made the statement:

"No Negro is improved by a visit to Columbia, & a visit to Charleston is his certain destruction."

Once the people had paid a visit to these places, they wanted to negotiate after having been there. The negotiations continued in order to truly establish themselves as not just "freedmen," but FREE MEN and women.

The paternalistic legal device called the "Black Codes" was established as a means to keep restrictions on enterprises and movements of people of African descent. This instrument also defined that 1/8 "Negro blood" made a person a "negro." "The Black Code was a special object of protest because it subjected the freedmen to penalties and restrictions that only applied to them. The economic disabilities were especially burdensome upon those who hoped to continue practicing trades, to develop business enterprises, or to acquire land. In addition, to these economic restrictions, exclusion from public schools limited their opportunities for social and intellectual improvement. In conclusion, the delegates declared that 'we simply desire that we shall be recognized as men; that we have no special obstructions placed in our way; that the same laws which govern white men shall direct colored men'." ("Black Charlestonians" p. 84)

Time and again the Gullah/Geechees and other people of African descent tried to appeal to some type of moral conscience to those that were the power brokers and lawmakers. One appeal was:

"We simply ask that we shall be recognized as men; that there be no obstructions placed in our way; that the same laws which govern white men shall govern black men; that we have the right of trial by jury or our peers; that schools be established for the education of colored children as well as white; and the advantages of both colors shall, in this respect, be equal; that no impediments be put in the way of our acquiring homesteads for ourselves and our people; that, in short, we be dealt with as others are-in equity and justice."

"The laws which have made white men powerful have degraded us, because we were black and because we were reduced to the conditions of chattels. But now that we are freedmen-now that we are elevated, by the Providence of God, to manhood, we have resolved to stand up, and like men, speak and act for ourselves. We fully recognize the truth of the maxim, 'The gods help those who help themselves."

During the 1960s, the sentiment of these words rang out again as James Brown sang, "I don't want nobody to give me nothin'. Open up the doe! I'll get it myself!"

These words were held up along side, "I know the one thing we did right was the day we started to fight! Keep your eyes on the prize. Hold on!" These words rang out from John's Island and infused the mainland as many marched arm and arm once again toward freedom and equity. Those that began protesting, sitting in, laying in, marching, singing and praying their demands were simply following in the footsteps of their ancestors that had done the same thing 100 years before.

Their ancestors had stood as a part of the group that gathered at the Charleston Clubhouse on Meeting Street on Tuesday, January 14, 1868. On this occasion, 76 black men who were mostly formerly enslaved met to make up a new constitution for the state of South Carolina.

Even laws have no effect if they are not enforced or systems of actual operations are in place to work against them. Thus, although the Emancipation Proclamation had been signed into law and celebrated, Jim Crow still did all he could to hold the doors to freedom closed. One of the locks was the attempt at keeping people segregated from use by people of African descent.

However, to prove that they also "had "a right to the tree of life," on March 27, 1867 Charleston demonstrators staged ride-ins on streetcars. In April 1867 police attempted to eject blacks from a car on the City Railway Company when they proposed to establish a partition between blacks and whites on the cars. This led to a riot.

This had not been the first riot in Charleston nor would it be the last. September 6, 1876 and May 10, 1919 race riots took place in Charleston. Over one hundred years later on March 10, 1969, civil rights workers took to the streets to assist hospital workers who went on strike. The Longshoreman's Union of Charleston has found itself marching numerous times over the years since its inception to support members that have been wrongly accused and even assaulted.

Gullah/Geechees have stood by their people through all of these situations. When some were arrested for the ride-ins, Gullah/Geechees forced themselves into the police station to release their people that were arrested. A month later the company decided against their plan to discriminate. On May 1, the *Charleston City Railway Company* adopted a resolution giving the right to all people to ride streetcars.

Armed with the spirit of freedom, Gullah/Geechees took part in their first public government election in 1868. They voted in the city elections of Charleston. Due to them being an active part of the process of change for the betterment of their people:

[In 1883] "Most public transportation was integrated, as it had always been. Some whites were now proposing that the State's civil rights law, which since the War had guaranteed equal rights, should be repealed, even though it was not being enforced. On November 5th the News and Courier published an editorial summarizing the situation and calling for moderation:

It is the custom all through the South to take colored nurses and other attendants into the first-class carriages, for the convenience of their employers. This has always been done. It has been the rule, also, for well-to-do colored persons, particularly women, to travel first-class. No trouble or discomfort has been complained of heretofore, on this score.

There has been little disposition on the part of the colored people generally to obtrude themselves upon the white people anywhere, and it would be altogether wrong to repeal the civil rights law until it is proved to be inconsistent with harmonious relations between the two races. The colored people have the same rights, under the Constitution of the State and of the United States, that the white people have. They do not seek social equality, which, in the end, would be hurtful to them as well as degrading to the white people." (Mazyk and Waddell "Charleston in 1883" p.xix)

Gullah/Geechees never saw receiving what was rightfully due to them as being hurtful in any way, especially not to themselves. Thus, they continued to gather, to strategize, and to pray that all that they had worked for and fought for would actually come into fruition from the tree of life. So, just as in the past, they got together in praise houses and churches and had a cry for freedom spring up from there just as their ancestors had even during Watch Night services in 1864 as they waited for Jubliee to finally come. The polyrhythmic hand claps with the rhythm of worn shoe soles hitting wood floors that held the blood, sweat, tears, and energy of those that had built these buildings with and through faith were the drums to signal the "uprising" or the "rising up" that was to come.

People were accustomed to going through the process of "seeking" and the "shouting" that would send folks into trance at praise meetings. All aspects of one "ketching hunnuh sense" had rules and regulations that were to be done "decently and in order." On Wadamalaw and all the other Sea Islands, there were praise houses. One descriptions for the process of becoming a member on Wadmalaw Island was written of as follows:

"And that Sunday night then they had to take me over into the Prayer House. I still couldn't, although I was baptized, go and sit on the front seat. Until these leaders, and one of the older sisters of the meeting house, come back there and git me and lead me on by my arms from the back bench to the front seat. Then I became a Christian. Now you go in church, you don't know who is a Christian from not a Christian. But at that time if you are not a Christian you had to sit on the back bench. You couldn't mix with the Christian people." (Johnson p. 12)

This aspect of separation had to do with the changed not simply continuing to mix with the spiritually unchanged and participate in the things that they had been doing. However, an underlying aspect of the praise house was always that they had to take community issues into a sacred space that had righteous energy surrounding the decisions that were to come forth from them. Gullah/Geechees firmly believed that just as God had made a way for the many oppressed people represented in the Bible, God would make a way for them also. "Trouble don' lass a'ways."

During enslavement, praise houses became daily gathering places. As time went on, meetings were held at these spaces weekly and some that continue to operate have gatherings monthly. They have more frequent gatherings and meetings at the churches. There are key times of year that Gullah/Geechees insure that they are in these sacred spaces to give praise and thanks for blessings no matter how hard times may seem.

Abraham Jenkins stated that *Moving Star Hall* on John's Island is where people of all denominations gathered for Christmas and New Year's. This is also the place from which the *Progressive*

Club began. According to Jenkins, "They used to have prayer service in the house-only family then. Afterward, they began to have joint class [class meeting] from house to house. Then when we get the hall, we begin to have meeting there.

My daddy teach we how to sing, teach we how to shout, teach we how to go fast, teach we how to go slow. And then going to meeting, or later going to church, he'll teach we how to behave yourself when we get out to different places before we leave home.

This description of the activities in the *Moving Star Hall* pray's house of Johns Island (which, incidentally, was not established until 1914) is true to the functions that these institutions have fulfilled in the South Carolina Lowcountry for more than a century." (Johnson and Jersild p. 9)

These institutions were the safe havens for many of the meetings that were held during the Civil Rights era. "Charleston in the 1950s was a segregated city. It ran a dual school system. Its hotels, restaurants, theaters, and recreational facilities adhered to strict codes separating the races. Signs told blacks where to sit on buses and from which water fountains they could drink. Like Greenville, Columbia, Augusta, Columbus, Macon, Savannah, Montgomery, Baton Rouge, Jackson, and so many other cities, Charleston had a color line that divided its people and institutions.

***Charleston was one of the last places where businessmen went home for a two o'clock dinner and a short nap before returning to work; it was also one of the places where virtually no white person thought of disturbing pre-existing roles between blacks and whites. Rules governing relationships between the races were etched in stone. The color line separated whites and blacks, assigning to each a different position in the social order and attaching to each position a different set of rights, privileges, and arenas of action..." (Smyth p. 99-100)

Esau Jenkins was one of the people that sought out his own way of crossing this color line. Esau was born on John's Island to Peter and Eva Campbell Jenkins on July 3, 1910 in a four room house on a farm on Bohicket Road on John's Island. Peter Jenkins was a farmer and carpenter. The couple had one other son who died when Esau was a baby.

Esau entered the one room school house at Legareville when he was seven years old. His mother passed away when he was nine. However, Mrs. Sarah Richardson helped his father take care of him.

Esau was unable to attend after four years since he had to help his father farm, but eventually taught himself to Greek and wanted to make sure that his children had the best education possible. He went to work on a boat in Charleston at one point making $1.25 per day, but he wanted to get more than the fourth grade education that he had, so he returned to school for four more years.

Jenkins returned to Johns Island in the 1930s and started farming for himself. He grew cotton for five years and then bought a truck. When he went to the market, he had to deal with a number of people that were Greek. Thus, he took up their language. Within two years, he was able to have a marketplace use of the language and it greatly assisted him with his business transactions. He would take his children to Burke on the peninsula in his truck each day. In 1945 he obtained a bus in order to take more children. Eventually, the county consented to pay him for this service. Once the school board realized that it was costing them a great deal to continue to pay for this service, they decided to build a consolidated school on the island. In 1952, *Haut Gap School* was built.

In 1948, he bought more buses. He would drive tobacco workers and longshoremen to work in Charleston. He taught adult passengers that rode the bus how to read as well. He taught them how to interpret the United States' Constitution so that they could become registered voters.

Esau Jenkins was the founder of the *"Progressive Club"* on River Road. Membership to the club was restricted to "registered citizens" (those that were registered to vote in United States and local elections). They met at *"Moving Star Hall"* every third Sunday and paid 25 cents dues. The money was used for bail for those that were often charged with insignificant things such as killing a white person's dog. The club formed a cooperative and opened their own grocery and gasoline store in an old school building that they purchased in 1957. The club was eventually moved to a larger building called the "Sea Island Center." Given that the *Progressive Club* was the only place where interracial groups could meet, it also got labeled as a communist headquarters.

The *Citizens' Committee* was started in 1959 to combat injustices, promote racial harmony throughout the county, and to provide scholarships to children. Since members believed that they were their brother's keepers, the non-profit totally operated from donations from individuals and businesses and through a $2 annual dues. Only residents of Charleston County could be members. Members of the committee were allowed to be members of the *C. O. Federal Credit Union*. The credit union was started on October 6, 1966 and eventually came to have 1700 members. It loaned out over a million dollars and had over a half million dollars in assets by the 1970s. In 1968 letter from Esau Jenkins to Howard Quander, Executive Council of the Episcopal Church Center who was headquartered in New York it was written:

"A few Black people in Charleston County are still singing folk songs and telling stories. Some people kid them about singing these songs and storytelling, but I asked them not to stop because these are part of our culture. It is our concern to keep these songs and stories because they have great religious back- ground and they are also telling messages.

We also would like to start a vocational school which will teach Black people how to repair televisions, radios, electric clocks, electric irons, and piccolos. We would also like to teach some carpentry, reading, and arithmetic.

Citizenships will be discussed in all classes, such as the importance of voter-registration, political education, and community pride which means fixing and painting up homes.

The Citizens' Committee's hopes that if we can do well in inspiring the rest of the Charleston County communities by this pilot project at the *Progressive Club of* John's Island of this king, the whole county could be much more independence [sic]; also be able to demand their labors, plus do a great deal of work for themselves."

Due to the encouragement of Anna Kelly and Septima Clark, Esau Jenkins spent two weeks at the *Highlander Folk School's United Nation Workshop* on race relations in 1954. From this experience he was able to obtain financial aide from Highlander for adult education classes to be conducted on Wadmalaw, John's and Edisto Islands.

In 1959, Esau Jenkins organized the "Citizens' Committee of Charleston County" which was responsible for the employment of black bus drivers by the *South Carolina Electric and Gas Company (SCE & G),* black truckers of the City Sanitation Department and the initiation of the war on poverty. From this committee came Head Start centers and the *C. O. Federal Credit Union* in October 1966.

Esau Jenkins also served as a Deacon and Superintendent of United Methodist Church of John's Island and Chairman of *Peace and World Order of the United Methodist Church* of Charleston District. He was on the board of directors of the *NAACP, Southern Christian Leadership Conference (SCLC), Christian Social Concern of United Methodist Church, Highlander Research Center, the Board of Trustees of School District Nine,* and the local board of *United Methodist Church and Rural Mission. The Rural Missions* came about as a result of a collaboration Jenkins did with the *Methodist's Church Women United* and Charlestonians such as Marybelle Howe and Mamie Garvin Fields. They worked together to provide basic social services including daycare and health programs to migrant workers. The Pastor Willis T. Goodwin, who is now a part of the staff of the *South Carolina World Trade Center* and also a member of the Assembly of Representatives for the Gullah/Geechee Nation, was the first director of *Rural Missions*. Rural Missions planned what would become the *Sea Island Comprehensive Health Center*, (This is the location of the annual *Sea Island Cultural Day* each September.) a nursing home, and a low-income housing project.

Esau Jenkins invested in a number of business enterprises including a fruit store on President Street and the J and P Motel on Spring Street. His wife, Janie Elizabeth Jones Jenkins, later operated the café. In 1950, he also opened a business at Atlantic Beach in the northern most area of the Gullah/Geechee Nation just outside of Myrtle Beach. He also had the "hot Spot Record Store" at 569 King Street. He was able to raise thirteen children from the income from these.

Esau's early life was what transformed his mind and set it on freedom. When he corrected a white man regarding an error when he was paying Esau's father for some crops, Esau's father told him that they don't like when you do that. Later Esau knew of more than once incident where black men were shot over incidents involving white people's dogs. One woman accused a man of "putting his dog on her dog." The man told her it was a lie so she told her husband who subsequently told the man to come out of the truck and then shot him with a shotgun. Fortunately, after several blood transfusions, the black man survived. However, this did not end these types of incidents. Another dog ran out in front of a truck and was killed and the white owner came out and killed the black man that had been driving the truck.

Another man was killed for kicking a dog. Jenkins died on Monday, October 30, 1972 at *McClennan-Banks Memorial Hospital* in Charleston, SC leaving a legacy of freedom and love.

Edisto Island had its share of civil rights fighters as well. Reverend McKinley Washington started *"Self-Development of People, Inc."* on the island. This organization brought job training programs, new jobs, Head Start, and day care to the community. The people of Edisto have not let Representative Washington's work go unrecognized. The bridge from the mainland to the islands has been named in his honor.

Were it not for many of the media instruments that were started and run by people of African descent, the work that "Black" people were doing for themselves would not have been acknowledged. These sources served as a means to get the truth about what was going on and who to support and who not to support out to the people. Today, Charleston has *"The Sentinel"* which comes out of Summerville and was started by Wendell and the *"Charleston Chronicle."* However, these newspapers follow in the historic line of *"The Charleston Lighthouse."* This was a black South Carolina newspaper was established in 1939.

John Henry McCray was the editor and publisher of the *Lighthouse and Informer*, South Carolina's leading black weekly newspaper in the 1940s and early 50s. McCray went on to become director of admissions and recruiter for *Talladega College* in Talladega, Alabama. He died in September 1987 at the age of 77.

Although McCray was born near Youngstown, Florida on August 25, 1910. His family moved from Youngstown to

Charleston, South Carolina, which was the birthplace of his mother. He went through the elementary schools in a town called Lincolnville, about twenty miles north of Charleston and later attended *Avery Institute* in Charleston and *Talladega College* in Talladega, Alabama.

Upon leaving college, he worked as the city editor of the *Charleston Messenger*, which was owned by the *Jenkin's Orphanage*. Since the management didn't want certain stories published, McCray started producing a newspaper of his own. The paper was a weekly called the *"Charleston Lighthouse."* In 1940, the newspaper was combined with the *People's Informer* out of Sumter, South Carolina. In 1941, the *Lighthouse and Informer* was published in Columbia, South Carolina in 1941. The paper closed down in 1954.

In an interview with McCray, he stated: *"I think the most important thing I hoped our newspaper could accomplish was recognition of blacks as a human beings. For example, no newspapers in South Carolina capitalized the word "Negro." You never saw a picture of a Negro in the daily newspaper unless it was somebody who had been arrested for a crime or something. Every year, the*

News and Courier published the statistics from the Charleston police department and every year followed this with an editorial calling attention to the fact that the largest number of arrests in Charleston were of blacks (even though the statistics didn't always bear this out). We undertook in our own way to correct that, and it worked very well."

Unfortunately, the main daily newspaper of Charleston has not corrected the types of stories that they print on a regular basis. The police force of Charleston's statistics have not changed a great deal either. The struggle for recognition of a people's history and their right to survive with a descent wage and a descent home and health care have not changed either.

So, often, *WPAL Radio* station continues to air such subjects on talk shows just as they did during the 1960s under the direction of Charleston's own Matthew Mounson who started running the station in 1968.

WPAL and many other media throughout the Gullah/Geechee Nation made sure that they would cover a history making event that marked the inception of the movement from civil rights to human rights. This event was the enstoolment ceremony held at Sullivan's Island on July 2, 2000. This was the first time that the Gullah/Geechee people had come together to declare themselves as their own nation. This ceremony to enstool Marquetta L. Goodwine as "Queen Quet" was the public confirmation of the election of her as the "head on the body" of the Gullah/Geechee Nation. She officially became the head of state, spokesperson and liaison for all Gullah/Geechee people on that day. The region from Jacksonville, North Carolina to Jacksonville, Florida encompassing all of the Sea Islands and thirty to thirty-five miles inland also officially became the Gullah/Geechee Nation.

The fact that this ceremony occurred on the same date that Denmark Vesey had been hung on and the fact that it was held at the same location that the enslaved Africans that blended to become the Gullah/Geechees came into did not happen by accident. It seemed to be Divinely Ordered that just where the enslavement began was where Nationhood had to begin. It seemed that it was time for the spirits that had been buried beneath the soil of the land and the omissions of the many books that had been written about the area had to come up just as seeds go into the soil to die in order to bring forth the life of new seeds.

The Gullah/Geechee fruits that have sprang forth from the seeds planted in "Cha'stun" have been spread around the world and they beat out freedom in polyrhythmic form as they march on in celebration of going from being called "nothing" and "nigger" to being a Nation!

Epilogue

From enslavement to sale to the Civil War to Reconstruction through the Jim Crow, Civil Rights, and Black Power eras to nationhood, Gullah/Geechees have endured a great deal. Families had to rebuild in Charleston and other places as family members crossed over into the realm of the ancestors due to gale wind storms in 1822, cholera in 1836, smallpox epidemics in 1848 and 1867, and the murders due to racism over the decades. These words of how they came to be and how they still stand are simply one brick on the monument of things that were accomplished in spite of the odds.

By no means have these pages mentioned all of the historic Gullah/Geechee events nor famous Gullah/Geechee Charlestonians. It would take volumes to accomplish that and more and more history is still being made there daily. However, this is my contribution to saluting a place that has accepted me at all times. It has acted as a womb for the Gullah/Geechee Nation to grow in acceptance by our people throughout the Gullah/Geechee Nation and throughout the world.

As Charleston continues to evolve and grow as a major hub of the continuation of the Gullah/Geechee culture, almost every community now has a community association that is focusing on their localized issues. Many of them have also developed small community functions as fundraisers and some like the *Edisto Island Community Association* have scholarship funds as well. There are numerous events that celebrate with the people:

Gullah/Geechee Nation

International African Music
&
Movement Festival
www.gullahgeechee.info

Gullah/Geechee Nation Headquarters
Post Office Box 1109
St. Helena Island SC 29920
(843) 838-1171
AMPTurnItUp@aol.com or GullGeeCo@aol.com
www.gullahgeecheenation.com

Sweetgrass Cultural Arts Festival
www.sweetgrassfestival.org

Moja Celebration
www.mojafestival.com

Blue Crab Festival
Last weekend of August in Awendaw, SC

Blessings of the Fleet
May in McClellanville, SC

Gullah/Geechee People Foundation Anniversary
(843) 572-6788

Sea Island Cultural Arts Day
September on John's Island at Comprehensive Health Center

Labor Day Parade and Celebration
Wadamalaw Island

These events are opportunities to link with the community that still lives the culture daily. These are times that they come together to laugh and share the joy of continuing to be who they are. They remain on the land that their ancestors cultivated and kept so that their future generations would always have a place on where they can grow and build.

Charleston, SC has emerged from being a place of devastation to being a place of commemoration and celebration. May the grounds of Charleston forever sing out and ring out the sounds emitted from the souls of the Africans whose blood sealed together the cobblestones. May Gullah/Geechees proudly stand upon these and be infused with the true spirit of FREEDOM!

Epilogue 2015

Since the first publication of this book, Charleston County has sought to honor the legacy of the Gullah/Geechees within these pages by being the first city to proclaim "Gullah/Geechee Nation Appreciation Week."

We also now have a statue of Denmark Vesey in downtown Charleston's Hampton Park.

There are historic markers at the Medical University of South Carolina (MUSC) in honor of the Charleston Hospital Workers' Strike and at the site of the Progressive Club on Johns Island, SC. Also, the door of Esau Jenkins' bus that he taught from and used during the Civil Rights Movement is now part of a permanent exhibition at the Smithsonian's National African American Museum in Washington, DC along with Phillip Simmons' gates, sweetgrass baskets, and various other Gullah/Geechee artifacts and historical items and images.

Bibliography

Abbott, Martin. "The Freedmen's Bureau and Its Carolina Critics." *The Proceedings of The South Carolina Historical Association*. Columbia, SC, 1962.

Anderson, James. *The Education of Blacks in the South 1860-1935*. University of North Carolina Press, Chapel Hill, NC, 1988.

Before Freedom Came : African-American Life in the Antebellum South. Museum Of The Confederacy University Press Of Virginia , 1991.

"Between Two Worlds: Christopher G Memminger of Charleston and the Old South in the Mid- Passage, 1830-1861." *The Proceedings of The South Carolina Historical Association*.

Columbia, SC, 1981."Blacks and the South Carolina Interstate and West Indian Exposition."

South Carolina Historical Magazine. Charleston, SC, October 1987.Brown, Richard Maxwell. *The South Carolina Regulators*. The Belknap Press of Harvard

University Press, Cambridge MA 1963.Burnside, Madeline and Rosemarie Robotham. *Spirits of the Passage: The Transatlantic Slave*

Trade in the Seventeenth Century. Simon & Schuster, New York, NY, 1887.

"Charleston's Free Afro-American Elite: The Brown Fellowship Society and the Humane Brotherhood." *The South Carolina Historical Magazine* Vol. 82 No. 4.

Charleston, SC, 1981.

Clifton, James. *"The Rice Driver: His Role in Slave Management"*

Creel, Margaret Washington. *A Peculiar People: Slave Religion and Community Culture Among the Gullahs.* New York University, 1988.

Eisterhold, John A. "Charleston: Lumber and Trade in a Declining Southern Port." *The South Carolina Historical Magazine* Vol. 74 No. 2. Charleston, SC., 1973.

Goodwine, Marquetta, ed. *The Legacy of Ibo Landing: Gullah Roots of African American Culture. Clarity Press, Inc.* Atlanta, GA, 1998.

Greene, Jack P. *Colonial South Carolina and the Caribbean Connection.*

Harding, Vincent. *There is a River: The Struggle for Freedom in America.* Harcourt Brace & Company, 1981.

Hicks, Teresa. "South Carolina Indians, Indian Traders, and Other Ethnic Connections Beginning in 1670." Reprint Company Publishers, Spartanburg, SC, 1998.

Jersild, Paul Jersild and Alonzo Johnson, ed. *Ain't Gonna Lay My 'Ligion Down: African American Religion in the South.* University of South Carolina Press. Columbia, SC, 1996.

Johnson, Guion Griffis. *A Social History of the Sea Islands.* University of North Carolina, Chapel Hill, NC, 1930.

Jones, George Fenwik. "The Black Hessians: Negroes

Recruited by the Hessians in South Carolina and Other Colonies."

Joyner, Charles. *Shared Traditions.* University of Illinois Press, Urbana and Chicago, 1999. Lamb, Martha J., ed. "How England Forced the Slave Upon America ." *Magazine of American*

History. New York, NY, July 1892.Leiding, Harriette Kershaw. *"Charleston Historic and Romantic."* J B Lippincott Company,

Philadelphia, PA, 1931. Littlefield, Daniel. "Charleston and Internal Slave Redistribution." *South Carolina Historical*

Magazine. Charleston, SC, April 1986.Litwack, Leon F. *Been in the Storm Too Long.* Random House Books, New York, 1979. Lofton, John, *Denmark Vesey Revolt.* Kent State University Press.

McFadden, Grace Jordan. "Oral Recollections as Mechanisms for Investigating the Social and Political Philosophy of Septima Poinsette Clark." *The Proceedings of The South Carolina Historical Association.* Columbia, SC, 1988.

McGowen, George S. "The Charles Town Board of Police, 1780-1782: A Study in Civil Administration under Military Occupation." *The Proceedings of The South Carolina Historical Association.* Columbia, SC, 1964.

Mazÿck, Arthur and Gene Waddell. *Charleston in 1883.* Southern Historical Press. Easley, SC, 1983.

Pine, W. M. "History Rides the Winds to Colonial

Charleston." *The South Carolina Historical Magazine* Vol. 87 No. 3. Charleston, SC, 1986.

Pope-Hennessy, James. *Sins of the Fathers: A Study of the Atlantic Slave Traders 1441-1807*. Barnes and Noble, Inc. New York, NY, 1988.

Powers, Bernard. *Black Charlestonians*. University of Arkansas Press, Fayetteville, AR, 1994.

Quarles, Benjamin. *The Negroes in the American Revolution*. University of North Carolina Press, Chapel Hill, NC, 1996.

Raboteau, Albert J. *Slave Religion*. Oxford University Press, Oxford, NJ, 1978. Rodriguez, Junius P. *Historical Encyclopedia of World Slavery*. ABC-CLIO, Santa Barbara, CA, 1997.

Rogers, George C. Jr. "Tribute to Henry Laurens." *The South Carolina Historical Magazine* 1991 Vol. 92 No. 4 Charleston, SC, 1991.

Satterthwaite, and Jones "Henry Laurens to Law." Donnan Documents, Wax, January 12, 1756.

Smith, Alice Huger. *A Carolina Rice Plantation of the Fifties*. William Morrow and Company New York, NY, 1936.

Smyth, William D Smyth. "Segregation in Charleston in the 1950s." *South Carolina Historical Magazine*. Charleston, SC, April 1991.

South Carolina Historical Magazine Volume 82. Charleston, SC, October 1981. *South Carolina Historical*

Magazine. "Renaming Charleston Rivers." Charleston, SC, January 1988.

Starobin, Robert S. *Denmark Vesey: the Slave Conspiracy of 1822*. Prentice-Hall Inc, Englewood Cliffs NJ.

Steen, Ivan D. "Charleston in the 1850s: As Described by British Travelers." *The South Carolina Historical Magazine* Vol. 71 No. 1. Charleston, SC, 1970.

Tindall, George Brown. *South Carolina Negroes 1877-1900*. University of South Carolina Press, Columbia, SC.

Tyler, Lyon G. "James Louis Petigru: Freedom's Champion in a Slave Society." *The South Carolina Historical Magazine* Vol. 83 No. 4. Charleston, SC 1982.

Van Houten, Abigail. "The Preservation of Freedmen's Cottages as a Physical Representation of African American History and Culture" Senior Thesis 2000

Vlach, John Michael. *Back to the Big House: The Architecture of Plantation Slavery*. University of North Carolina Press Chapel Hill, NC, 1993.

Williams, Jack k. "The Southern Movement to Reopen the African Slave Trade, 1854-1860: A Factor in Secession. *The Proceedings of The South Carolina Historical Association,* Columbia, SC, 1960

Resource Locations

The majority of the documents that were reviewed for this book came from the following archives:

**Gullah/Geechee Sea Island Coalition Alkebulan Archive International University of the Gullah/Geechee
www.gullahgeechee.net**

www.gullahgeecheenation.com

**Avery Research Center for African American Culture
125 Bull Street**

Charleston SC

Phone: (843) 953-7609 Fax: (843) 953-7607
www.cofc.edu/avery

About the Author

Queen Quet Marquetta L. Goodwine is the head-of-state for the Gullah/Geechee Nation. Queen Quet, Chieftess of the Gullah/Geechee Nation stems from two Gullah/Geechee families of Dataw, Polowana, and St. Helena Island, South Carolina where she was homegrown in her native culture. She is the first selected and elected Queen Mother, official spokesperson, and liaison for the Gullah/Geechee Nation. She was the first Gullah/Geechee to speak on behalf of her people at the United Nations in Genevé, Switzerland.

Queen Quet has spent her life teaching the world about her people the Gullah/Geechees that reside from Jacksonville, North Carolina to Jacksonville, Florida on all of the Sea Islands and thirty to thirty-five miles inland onto the mainland. This region often referred to as the "Lowcountry" and northeastern Florida continues to be the homeland of this unique African culture, the Gullah language, and its dialect, Geechee.

This is the fifth volume of the thirty volume series called "Gullah/Geechee: Africa's Seed in the Winds of the Diaspora." This volume takes the reader on a journey from the entry of enslaved Africans into Sullivan's Island in Charleston, South Carolina to the establishment of the Gullah/Geechee Nation which was recognized at this same point of entry. The souls that scream from beneath the concrete of Charleston have had their words, trials, and triumphs scribed in this particular work. They have gone from the auction block to nationhood.

WEBE Gullah/Geechee Anointed People!"

Made in the USA
Charleston, SC
04 March 2015